working with
PEOPLE

CMI

Chartered Manager

Transform the way you work

The Chartered Management Institute's Chartered Manager award is the ultimate accolade for practising professional managers. Designed to transform the way you think about your work and how you add value to your organisation, it is based on demonstrating measurable impact.

This unique award proves your ability to make a real difference in the workplace.

Chartered Manager focuses on the six vital business skills of:

- Leading people
- Managing change
- Meeting customer needs
- Managing information and knowledge
- Managing activities and resources
- Managing yourself

Transform your organisation

There is a clear and well-established link between good management and improved organisational performance. Recognising this, the Chartered Manager scheme requires individuals to demonstrate how they are applying their leadership and change management skills to make significant impact within their organisation.

Transform your career

Whatever career stage a manager is at Chartered Manager will set them apart. Chartered Manager has proven to be a stimulus to career progression, either via recognition by their current employer or through the motivation to move on to more challenging roles with new employers.

instant manager
skills for success

CMI

working with
PEOPLE

SIDNEY CALLIS

HODDER
EDUCATION
PART OF HACHETTE LIVRE UK

The publisher has used its best endeavours to ensure that the URLs for external websites referred to in this book are correct and active at the time of going to press. However, the publisher and the author have no responsibility for the websites and can make no guarantee that a site will remain live or that the content will remain relevant, decent or appropriate.

Orders: Please contact Bookpoint Ltd, 130 Milton Park, Abingdon, Oxon OX14 4SB. Telephone: (44) 01235 827720, Fax: (44) 01235 400454. Lines are open from 9.00 to 5.00, Monday to Saturday, with a 24-hour message answering service. You can also order through our website www.hoddereducation.co.uk.

British Library Cataloguing in Publication Data
A catalogue record for this title is available from the British Library.

ISBN-13: 978 0340 947364

First published   2010
Impression number   10 9 8 7 6 5 4 3 2 1
Year   2013 2012 2011 2010

Typeset by Transet Limited, Coventry, England.
Printed in Great Britain for Hodder Education, an Hachette Livre UK Company, 338 Euston Road, London NW1 3BH, by Cox & Wyman, Reading, Berkshire RG1 8EX.

Hachette Livre UK's policy is to use papers that are natural, renewable and recyclable products and made from wood grown in sustainable forests. The logging and manufacturing processes are expected to conform to the environmental regulations of the country of origin.

But don't take just our word for it ...

Chartered Manager has transformed the careers and organisations of managers in all sectors.

- *'Being a Chartered Manager was one of the main contributing factors which led to my recent promotion.'*
  Lloyd Ross, Programme Delivery Manager, British Nuclear Fuels

- *'I am quite sure that a part of the reason for my success in achieving my appointment was due to my Chartered Manager award which provided excellent, independent evidence that I was a high quality manager.'*
  Donaree Marshall, Head of Programme Management Office, Water Service, Belfast

- *'The whole process has been very positive, giving me confidence in my strengths as a manager but also helping me to identify the areas of my skills that I want to develop. I am delighted and proud to have the accolade of Chartered Manager.'*
  Allen Hudson, School Support Services Manager, Dudley Metropolitan County Council

- *'As we are in a time of profound change, I believe that I have, as a result of my change management skills, been able to provide leadership to my staff. Indeed, I took over three teams and carefully built an integrated team, which is beginning to perform really well. I believe that the process I went through to gain Chartered Manager status assisted me in achieving this and consequently was of considerable benefit to my organisation.'*
  George Smart, SPO and D/Head of Resettlement, HM Prison Swaleside

To find out more or to request further information please visit our website **www.managers.org.uk/cmgr** or call us on **01536 207429**.

For Bim – for everything.

Contents

CHAPTER 08

CHAPTER 09

CHAPTER 10

CHAPTER 11

CHAPTER 12

Foreword

There has never been a greater need for better management and leadership skills in the UK. As we've seen over the past couple of years, it's all too often the case that management incompetence takes the blame for high-profile, costly and sometimes tragic failures. Put this in the context of a world dominated by changing technology and growing international competition, and every manager in this country has a responsibility for ensuring that he or she has the best possible skills to contribute to successful business performance.

So it is alarming that just one in five managers in the UK are professionally qualified. The truth is that we spend less on management development in the UK than our European competitors. Effectively this means that, if you want to develop professionally, if you want to boost your career chances, or if you just want recognition for the work you do, the onus is on you – the individual – to improve your skills. What it also means is that all of us – individual managers, employers and policy makers – need to answer difficult questions about how well equipped we are to lead in the 21st century. Are our standards slipping? How capable are we when it comes to meeting the skill requirements of modern business? Studies show that project management, alliance-building and communication skills are the three key 'over-arching' skills that must be mastered by the successful manager. But how many people can honestly claim they have mastery over all three?

In recent years the news has been dominated by stories focusing on breathtaking management failures. The collapse of the banking sector has been much-analysed and will continue to be discussed in the years to come. It's not just the private sector. Vast amounts of column inches have been devoted to investigations of failures across the health and social care sector, too. The spotlight has also been on management, at an individual level, as the recession deepened in the aftermath of the banking crisis, with dramatic rises in the UK's unemployment levels. Many managers are fighting an ongoing battle to control costs and survive with reduced credit and slowing demand. They are also struggling to prove their worth, to show they meet required standards now, and in the long-term.

But imagine a world where management and leadership enables top-class performance right across British businesses, the public sector and our not-for-profit organisations – where management isn't a byword for bureaucracy and failure, but plays a real role in boosting performance. The way to achieve such a realistic utopia is by developing the skills that will help you, as a manager, perform to the best of your capability. And that is why this book will help. Its aim is to provide you with practical, digestible advice that you can take straight from the pages to apply in your working environment.

Does any of this matter? Well, you wouldn't want your accounts signed off by someone lacking a financial qualification. You certainly wouldn't let an unqualified surgeon anywhere near you with a scalpel, nor would you seek an unqualified lawyer to represent your interests. Why, then, should your employer settle for management capability that is second best? It means that you need to take time out to develop your skills so that these can be evaluated and so you can stand out from the competition.

What's more, managers will play a critical role in determining how well the UK meets a wide range of challenges over the next decade. How can managers foster innovation to promote economic growth? How do they tackle the gender pay gap and the continued under-representation of women in the boardroom, as part of building truly fair, diverse organisations? Managers in all sectors will need to learn how to lead their teams through the changes we face; they will also need to be able to manage change. Above all, managers will need to grasp the nettle when it comes to managing information and knowledge. The key will rest in how they learn to manage themselves.

First-class management and leadership really can drive up both personal and corporate performance. It can boost national productivity and enhance social wellbeing. If you want to be the best manager you can be, this book is for you. In one go it will provide you with practical advice and the experience of business leaders. It is also a fascinating and enthralling read!

Ruth Spellman OBE
Chief Executive
Chartered Management Institute

Acknowledgements

This book could not have been written without the help of dozens of colleagues, many hundreds of students and innumerable people in business, both in management and on the shopfloor! I learned from them, over many years, how to work with people, and how to pass on learning. I learned how different cultures work all over the world from South East Asia to South America, from East Africa to Eastern Europe and – occasionally – in Britain. I learned that all have one thing in common – all are human beings, with hopes, aspirations, fears and feelings. To work together well you need to get to know and understand each other. Whatever it is that we do, we want and need to achieve our goals. And we will not get there unless we work together in at least some sort of harmony.

There have, of course, been difficult times in my own journey, and I have been fortunate to have had mentors and consultants to help me out. It would be invidious to name names, but they will know who they are, and recognise their teachings in this book. And there have been books too, instructive and inspirational, which have given me insights into why people behave as they do. The best way to work together with people is to work *with* them, learn from them, and let them learn from you. I hope this book will help you along the way.

01

Introduction

Management is a relatively recent phenomenon. A definition might be: 'managing is getting things done through people'. Bosses get things done, often without consulting people at all. But management implies that people matter. People work better, produce more and cause less trouble if they are treated with consideration of their humanity. Today we are involved in a highly organised, sophisticated system that expends a vast amount of time, energy and other resources in 'getting things done through people'. Nowadays people count; they are the most important resource in any enterprise. People matter – which is what this book is about: working with people.

Objectives and methodology for working effectively with people

The process of getting things done is arranged in a similar way, whatever the field of endeavour: from the armed forces to scientific research. Someone is chief; someone reports (i.e. is commanded by) to them; a further someone reports to the second in command and so on, right down to the tea lady. Somewhere in this organisation you fit – a manager, albeit with less responsibility or authority than the boss, but nonetheless charged with getting things done. These 'things' may be defined, closely or loosely or perhaps not at all. It is a very good idea to have what you do defined by an organisation chart and job description. The big boss has ultimate responsibility for everything in the organisation; your responsibility is for a specified small area. This is why it is so important to have a clear statement of responsibilities and authority; without this you may not be able to perform effectively. Sadly this clear statement is often missing.

So you are part of the chain of management, and it is a difficult part. Above is the boss, who may not have, or may not have been able to, exactly specify the job. Below are the workers, your people who expect guidance and direction. Have you had any training for this?

Managing other people is a technique (art? wizardry? science?) that can be taught and learned. In this book we deal with the essential things of everyday working life at the sharp end. The things you need to know concern the technical aspects of getting the job done and how best to get people to do it. The first things to understand are where you fit, what your role is, and how your own personal leadership can be developed. Without an understanding of these elements any manager will be on shaky ground. Knowing what your work responsibilities are helps you deal with the job effectively. Having a good idea of what leadership is about will enable you to put some of the principles into practice and self develop – and also develop your people.

Then there is what this book is about: the nuts and bolts of everyday management, planning, controlling and problem solving. These things are a structural part of any manager's daily work. Everybody plans to some extent, but you have to plan not just for your own activity, but for the team as well and also to meet the objectives of the organisation. This can be complex; integrating all the interests that are involved needs skill and determination. Then, it is essential to ensure that the plans are carried out; that the results planned for have actually happened. This again requires skill because, in working with people, the idea of control can often be distasteful to some.

Solving problems is what the manager is most concerned with. It takes time, which often is not a good expenditure of this valuable resource. You need to be available to help with problem solving, whether it is a technical problem or a personal one. But your attitude should be 'don't bring me problems, bring me answers'. In other words, don't ask me to solve a problem that you can really solve yourself; think about it a bit before running to me. In working with people one of your main jobs is to encourage people to learn to think for themselves, to develop initiative and solve their own problems as far as possible.

We have a job to do, in a specific amount of time; we need to plan and control what we are doing, so that excessive problem solving does not hold us up.

The thinking manager will adapt their management style to the circumstances and call up their leadership, planning and control skills. Also, good communication is vital. One important aspect of management style is the extent to which you are able/willing to delegate. Effective delegation opens the greatest possibilities for collaboration and extends your capabilities, as well as developing people. If they are accustomed to extended delegation, they will be much more attuned to the difficulties of making changes than those who simply accept orders.

The art of management is intricately tied up with the techniques of getting things done and using people to do things. Management is a structure of many parts; leave out one, or ignore, or miss, a piece and the thing goes lopsided. It may work, but not efficiently. Instead of a well-oiled machine that performs to specification, one may have a creaky ill-tempered beast that needs constant attention and adjustment to make it go at all. The thinking manager will do well to acquire and practise good management skills, including effective ways of working with people.

The ability to communicate effectively is one of the most potent skills that any individual can have in life. In your job you need to communicate both up to senior management and down to your people; having such skill is a great asset. Communication skills can be learned, but they need a lot of determination and persistent practice. We talk mostly about spoken communication because this is the most used in your work: giving instructions; discussing plans or activity; making a presentation to explain, or to convince people about change. Most of this is the spoken word. But you must also be skilled in the written word: for reports to be made, or plans to be drawn up and so on. This needs clarity of expression in writing, whether this be on paper, via an email, fax or any other electronic method, or even as a text message! And there are other skills that you would do well to acquire: how to read body language; how to conduct a meeting effectively; questioning techniques to get the information that one needs; and learning to listen. This skill is almost more important than speaking, or writing in a management context (or in life – apparently it is difficult for men to listen, less so for women!).

Without good communication skills the quality of the manager's job will inevitably be less than optimum. Effectiveness will be measurably enhanced with improvement in communication skill. You have to deal with other people; it is thus important to understand what motivates people and how and why they form relationships. It is also helpful in the work situation to be able to perceive what people expect of us and, even more, what we expect of them – and how we show or express this. A level of sensitivity is called for to appreciate what motivates ourselves and those with whom we work. Well-motivated people perform well; it is our job to ensure that the level of motivation is high and that relationships within the work environment are smooth. Ruffled feathers spell trouble; low morale and poor motivation means poor results in your work area. The figures do not lie: if there is a downturn in productivity look for the causes, not in machine or materials failure, but in people failures.

This is where the manager's role as coach can have such a significant impact. Any person in a supervisory capacity accumulates a store of knowledge, wisdom and people skills. To make a difference all these can be brought to bear in the process of coaching and helping: 'Let me help you do it' but not 'Let me do it for you'. The coach combines the functions of demonstrator, observer, commentator, evaluator and praiser. In all these areas you as coach have the experience to guide individuals to satisfactory performance.

The chapters of this book deal with various aspects of management. But important though these subjects are, there are many more areas that you should know about, but which will have little impact on the work, and which you will not be able to influence directly.

You should have some understanding of: finance, a vast and terrifying area for some; marketing, an arcane jungle; production; procurement; industrial relations and law, and much more. All this buzzes around the concept of 'management'. And to supplement this are the latest fads, gimmicks and techniques dreamed up by consultants and academics in business schools, which often have no relevance or reality: 'Total Quality Management'; 'Corporate Re-engineering', to name but a couple of the most recent. The fads come and go; they flourish, then wither, then the next one arrives. You may be involved in the upheavals (change or chaos?) and that is part of the job. But the fundamentals remain; they may get called by fancy names for some time but they nevertheless remain the basics of the manager's job.

Before you read any further it might be a good idea to take stock: of what you know about, how you fit in, and your job. Obviously whatever you put into the following questionnaire remains private. However, the most interesting thing is what you don't put in, i.e. what you don't know. It could really be worthwhile to fill in those gaps.

It is NOT an exam! There are no right or wrong answers – only what you know. If you don't know anything about a particular point, just leave it blank. This could be an incentive for you to find out.

Self organisation – some ideas

To work with people effectively, you really need to be organised, and organisation means self-discipline. This is hard! The following ideas may be helpful and they rely very much on practising the Pareto principle firmly. (We will explain this principle later on, but essentially it means dealing first with the important things and then looking after the trivia.)

- Make a 'To Do' list daily. Do this last thing before leaving in the evening or first thing in the morning. It will pay off! Categorise tasks into:
  - Urgent
  - Important
  - Then prioritise.
- Be realistic – you can only do so much in one day. If you have tasks left over, carry them forward, re-prioritise. If you have carried them forward more than three times, chuck them out – they don't need doing!
- Do not fill every minute with activities – allow for the unexpected (which will happen!). Review your list frequently and reorganise as needed. Try to calculate the amount of time each task will take.
- Before doing each task ask yourself:
  - 'Why me?'
  - Can someone else do this? An excellent opportunity for some delegation.
- Group related activities together so as to concentrate your own and your team's efforts.
- Work on key tasks every day: focus on outcomes, grade the urgency.
- Think ahead constantly. Don't neglect tasks you don't like so they eventually become urgent (and therefore a crisis).

Questionnaire – what do you know?

Where do you fit in?

1 To whom are you immediately responsible? Title _____

2 To whom do you report in their absence? Title _____

3 Can you trace the line of authority from yourself to the top
   and bottom of the company?   Yes ☐ No ☐

4 Is the line clear?   Yes ☐ No ☐

5 How many people are responsible to you? Number: _____

6 Is this a manageable number?   Yes ☐ No ☐

7 If no, what can you do about it?

   _____

   _____

8 Do you have regular contact with your own manager?
                                                  Yes ☐ No ☐

9 Do you have a deputy who acts in your absence?
                                                  Yes ☐ No ☐

10 Do you meet with your fellow managers regularly?
                                                  Yes ☐ No ☐

11 Do you know and work with the specialists in your company?

          Personnel ☐   Training ☐   Accounts ☐

others: _____ _____ _____ _____

(tick those known, add others.)

Is this your job?   **Yes   No**

1 Determining the number of people required
   in your section.   ☐   ☐

                                                   (Continued)

		Yes	No
2	Selecting new people.	☐	☐
3	Induction of new people.	☐	☐
4	Training people on the job.	☐	☐
5	Authorising leave of absence.	☐	☐
6	Arranging overtime.	☐	☐
7	Recommending merit awards.	☐	☐
8	Ensuring compliance with relevant company and statutory regulations.	☐	☐
9	Keeping various records.	☐	☐
10	Doing personnel appraisals.	☐	☐
11	Suggesting improved methods of working.	☐	☐
12	Keeping a check on costs and wastage.	☐	☐
13	Checking work.	☐	☐
14	Upgrading performance.	☐	☐
15	Keeping an eye on adequacy and effectiveness of furniture and equipment.	☐	☐
16	Supervising maintenance, cleaning and storage of items.	☐	☐
17	Keeping up to date with new ideas and new equipment and recommending their use where advisable.	☐	☐
18	Controlling the flow of work through your section.	☐	☐
19	Maintaining an effective working team.	☐	☐
20	Planning for the future.	☐	☐
21	Making decisions about technical, organisational and people problems.	☐	☐

Looking at this list, is your workload:

	Yes	No
Too much?	☐	☐
Too little?	☐	☐
Enough to keep you busy without stress?	☐	☐
Do you feel you have: adequate knowledge?	☐	☐
Do you feel you have sufficient training to do the job?	☐	☐

Think about what you have put in the questionnaire. Do you feel you know enough about your job? If you have left spaces unanswered then, as you read through this book, maybe they will be filled in. Or maybe you will feel the need to go and find some answers. Good hunting!

SUMMARY

This chapter has introduced the overall theme of the book. Managers work with people to fulfil the objectives of the organisation, whatever they may be. They are the key links in the chain from intentions to results. Some of the things that managers need to do are outlined very briefly in this chapter. For example: problem solving, delegation, leadership and, above all, communication in all its forms.

No matter what your title is, or how exalted or lowly in the organisation, your job is to get things done through people. Absorbing the wisdom contained in this book will help you get that job done – well!

02

How do we communicate?

Good communication is at the heart of working with people effectively. To do your job you need to ensure that you – and your people – know what needs to be done. This means good understanding of what is happening from both sides. You all need information; the best way to get this is to communicate well. If you, as the leader, show good communication by example, then you will be exhibiting leadership skills; by really listening you will be empathising with your people, showing you understand. You will be taking them into your confidence, consulting with them and getting the sort of feedback that will enable all of you to do an excellent job.

But good communication is difficult; every person you deal with is different and has different expectations. As a manager you will come into contact with a wide range of people. You need to be able to handle them well, give good service, give yourself satisfaction and avoid stress.

Developing working relationships with colleagues

Getting along with others

Here are some practical ideas to help you get along with people.

- Don't say everything you think.
- Make few promises but, if you want to be trusted, keep the ones you make.
- Praise good work, no matter who did it.
- Show and have empathy. Put yourself in the other person's place.
- Keep an open mind. If you are the only one coming up with the 'right' answers, something is wrong. Discuss, don't argue.
- Let your good points speak for themselves; but be ready to discuss them when asked.
- Do not talk about anyone else's weaknesses unless absolutely necessary, and never embarrass another person publicly.
- Watch your body language; it may say more than you intend or want to say.
- Treat everybody as if they were important.
- In all cases 'before opening mouth, engage brain!'

Be positive

You want to be seen as someone who gets the job done, so respond with 'I will' or 'I can' as often as possible. But watch this; avoid the overload situation. Learn to say 'No' pleasantly also. And remember that phrases such as 'I'll try' make you appear weak.

Think about all the people who say 'I'll try to get back to you tomorrow'. They seldom do. Those, however, who say 'I'll have an answer for you by five' usually follow through.

Your attitude and choice of words will influence others; it will also influence you to get the job done. You have made a sort of contract with yourself – so you'll do it – as promised. People will respect you and so be easier to work with.

Handling tough conversations

To avoid potential stress for you and those you are dealing with, try to avoid confrontation. In a potential tough conversation:

- Begin with agreement, start off your discussion with some area on which you both easily agree. Even if it is very small and requires real digging to uncover common ground, do it.
- Say 'and' – not 'but'. 'But' acts like an eraser inside people's heads. It seems to devalue anything said before it.

Use lots of 'I' statements. Limit 'you' statements. 'I' in a way asks the other for help, allows you to appear vulnerable and shows you as a person. 'I' clarifies what you think and feel; 'you' can make a person feel criticised. 'I' will also reduce defensiveness and help improve communication and avoid conflict.

Also avoid negative and absolute statements.

Negative:　　'Why can't you......'
Positive:　　'What if we......'

Negative:　　'I hate it when ...'
Positive:　　'Perhaps it would be better if ...'

Absolute: 'He always says ...'
Non-absolute: 'I've heard him say ...'

Absolute: 'Nothing ever gets done right around here.'
Non-absolute: 'At times, we've had problems getting things done correctly.'

Absolute: 'We must do it this way.'
Non-absolute: 'Here's a good idea to consider.'

Asking the right questions

To get constructive answers, make sure your questions are strong and directive. Weak questions use non-specific language and get imprecise answers..

Weak: 'Are you pleased with your progress so far?'
Strong: 'Where do you plan to go from here in the project; how do you see yourself accomplishing your goals?'

Weak: 'Can you learn complex processes quickly?'
Strong: 'What kind of process do you feel you can learn best?'

Weak: 'Do you find it easy to work with your staff?'
Strong: 'Do you and your people think alike? How do you differ?'

Weak: 'Do you work well with people?'
Strong: 'How did you handle an important relationship you had to maintain?'

Weak: 'Can you take criticism?'
Strong: 'How do you react when someone criticises you?'

Weak: Can you make decisions?'
Strong: 'What do you do when you have to make an important decision?'

By asking strong, clear, direct questions that invite a reply in detail (open questions) you get good discussion and a fuller understanding of the other person's point of view.

Dealing with a 'know-it-all'

When dealing with a 'know-it-all', don't attempt to be a know-it-all in return. These are awkward people whose attitude often covers an inner insecurity. When you disagree, they will often freeze their plans and will not budge. Then you have created a standoff.

What to do
For example, instead of telling a 'know-it-all' why their idea won't work, ask questions about the idea; they love to answer questions – it bolsters their ego. As they look for answers, they might just discover that some ideas you present could be useful. Indeed, they will probably blend some of your ideas with theirs and think they came up with all of them. You are doing well if you can make people think that what you have said is their idea.

Defensiveness

If communication is poor or even fails, people become defensive (and this could mean going on the attack) or self-protective. This is no good for business. It could happen in several ways. Remember you are the manager and, in general terms, poor communication is your fault. If you upset people through poor communications you seriously damage your chances of good relationships and the prospect of them co-operating with you will diminish.

● You may be being ambiguous, or your motivation may be unclear to the other person or the group.
● You may be speaking in a way to imply blame or making prejudiced statements.
● You may be speaking in a way to control the other person or the group. This could cause the others to perceive themselves as of little worth, especially if you talk with little warmth or caring for the listeners.
● You may be talking in a way perceived to be 'superior' to others; this may arouse feelings of inadequacy in the listeners.
● You may be talking dogmatically or with perceived certainty. This almost certainly will result in feelings of inferiority in the listener. You are always 'right'; if they disagree they are 'wrong'.

These errors in communication do a lot of damage to motivation, and cause difficulties in working with people.

Listening

Listening plays a vital role in our everyday communications, it affects everything we do. But most people operate at only about a quarter of their listening efficiency. This inefficiency is a constant cause of problems in working with people.

To become good listeners we have to overcome major stumbling blocks: learn listening techniques, watch speakers' non-verbal actions, and listen for emphasis within the message. In our formal education, reading and writing skills were emphasised, but the skills of speaking and listening were assumed to be there; these background skills were not polished.

Listening is not as simple as might be expected. Some people don't want to, or won't, listen; when people fail to hear and understand each other the results are costly. Tests have shown that after a 10-minute presentation, the average listener hears, receives, comprehends and retains only about half of any given message. After 48 hours most listeners only remember about a quarter of what they heard. To improve listening skills, we must identify and overcome barriers. You can listen faster than the speaker can speak. The average speaking rate is about 125 words per minute; your capacity to listen is about 400–600 words a minute. Therefore, while you are listening, you have a lot of time free. Use this extra time to improve your understanding of what is being said, think up answers, make decisions, and plan suggestions.

Here are some ideas to overcome obstacles and improve listening:

- Don't waste listening time.
- The burden of listening is on the listener. Don't automatically condemn a speaker or the subject as uninteresting.
- Don't prejudice your listening because you don't like the speaker's looks, voice, etc.
- Whatever you feel about the speaker or subject, hear the speaker out first.
- Don't let your eyes wander or your head turn about aimlessly.
- Don't drum your fingers or mindlessly handle pens and so on.
- Facts are important, but only as stepping stones leading to a major point.
- Don't keep your mind so occupied with bits of information that you miss the speaker's overall message.
- Jot down highlights or key ideas; pay more attention to hearing the message than to writing everything down.
- Don't pretend to be receiving the message while your mind has made a mental detour and is busy with different ideas.

As well as identifying and overcoming obstacles to effective listening, follow these six guidelines to improve listening efficiency.

1. **Look at the person speaking** This shows interest. Don't stare. People often do not trust a person who won't look at them – distrust blocks communication.

2. **Ask questions** This is the best way to become a better listener quickly. Direct questions discover facts that give specific, concise answers. Open-ended questions enable you to find out most of the information you need. But nobody likes to feel they are being interrogated, so have a purpose to each question, and ask them in a polite and courteous way.

3. **Don't interrupt** Do not jump into the middle of a conversation when you get an idea or are reminded of something by someone else's words. Practise letting other people finish their sentence or ideas before interrupting.

4. **Don't change the subject** The person who was cut off may not offer any more ideas. They will probably find a reason to get away from the interrupter, who also changed the subject.

5. **Emotions** People may get angry or excited by certain subjects. Curb your emotions and control your urge to interrupt and express your opinion. Try to understand the speaker first, then present your ideas in a controlled manner.

6. **Responsiveness** Let the speaker know you are interested. Most people will not go on talking for long unless we are responsive and offer some sign of understanding.

Keys to effective listening

Here are some guidelines to develop better listening habits:

No.	Effective Listening Traits	The Poor Listener	The Effective Listener
1.	Finds areas of interest.	Tunes out boring subjects (his perception).	Is an opportunist; asks 'what's in it for me?'
2.	Judges content, not delivery.	Tunes out if delivery is poor.	Judges content; doesn't worry about errors of delivery.
3.	Holds fire.	Gets into arguments.	Doesn't judge until he has complete comprehension.
4.	Listens for ideas.	Listens for facts.	Listens for central themes.
5.	Is flexible.	Takes intensive notes; uses only one system.	Takes fewer notes. Uses different systems, depending on speaker.
6.	Works at listening.	Shows no energy output. Attention is faked.	Works hard, exhibits active body state.
7.	Resists distractions.	Distracted easily.	Fights or avoids distractions, tolerates bad habits, knows how to concentrate. *(Continued)*

No.	Effective Listening Traits	The Poor Listener	The Effective Listener
8.	Exercises mind.	Resists difficult material; seeks light, recreational material.	Uses heavier material as exercise for the mind.
9.	Keeps mind open.	Reacts to emotional words.	Interprets colours, words; does not get hung up on them.
10.	Capitalises on the fact that thought is faster than speech.	Tends to daydream with slow speakers.	Challenges, anticipates, mentally summarises, weighs the evidence, listens between the lines to tone of voice.

Use questions

There are various kinds of questions that you can use to get a full exchange of views between people. In many situations, especially in boss/subordinate ones, people are often hesitant or even fearful; this can happen on both sides. The closed question that simply gets a 'yes' or 'no' answer is appropriate sometimes. But it doesn't get you very far if you are either trying to persuade, or get ideas or agreement from someone.

The following types of questions can be used to stimulate verbal communication:

Open questions

An open question cannot be answered 'yes' or 'no'. It invites a true expression of opinion and feelings, whether they are favourable or unfavourable to your point of view, for example:
'What do you think of...?'
'How do you feel about...?'

There are several advantages to using open questions:

- They show your interest in the other person. We like having others interested in us and what we think.
- They make the other person more comfortable and secure. They allow them to direct the conversation for a time.
- They get them to think about your ideas.
- They draw them out and let you learn more about them, and what's on their mind. The answers tell you where the real blocks to agreement are; you can design your approach more effectively.

Reflective questions

Reflective questions are the repetition or rephrasing, in your own words, of what the other person is trying to say or seems to feel. It is essential to listen carefully and select. To reflect feelings properly, really **listen**, don't think about your own plan or what you are going to say next. Then, select the most important idea or feeling from what has been said, and put it into your own words. Reflection does several things:

- It avoids argument; it enables you to respond without either rejecting or accepting what has been said.

- It shows that you understand. If your reflection is wrong, they have a chance to correct you. This goes a long way towards creating mutual understanding. There is also the ploy of the 'deliberate mistake'. Reflect incorrectly, they then correct you. This deepens understanding on both sides.
- The sharing of feelings creates a climate of agreement.
- If they have been illogical they will be able to see the error better when it is expressed by you. Getting the other person to correct their own mistakes relieves you of this responsibility. It also avoids creating friction between you.
- A bad idea is very often forgotten after you have reflected it back. In hearing it from you, the errors can be recognised.
- Reflection enables people to pick up the main idea, they can then continue a logical progression in their thinking.
- Reflection encourages people to express themselves further, or clarify something they have previously said.

Directive questions

Directive questions request expansion or further explanation on one particular point. Hold directive questions off until you have had a complete expression of feelings and opinions, so that you understand the other person's point of view as much as possible. Directive questions keep two-way communication going, and also get clarification of some things in which you are directly interested.

- They give you more information about their thinking on points where you need such information.
- They tend to make them more favourable to your position. The more you get the other person to explore the area of agreement, the less important the area of disagreement will seem.

● They give the other person the opportunity to convince themselves. By getting them to concentrate on the positive factors, they will often realise that it is to their advantage to accept your ideas.

Redirect questions

These are a very useful, if impertinent, type of question. Simply ask, in reply to a negative statement 'Why not?' or 'Why can't we do this?' This pushes the other person into thinking about the problem again; it may relieve a deadlock. It could end up in more fruitful discussion, where both sides may be able to change their minds and get agreement.

Written or spoken communication?

Remember to balance the relative advantages and disadvantages of the written and the spoken word for your communication. Some people prefer to see things in writing, to think about them before having a discussion. Others prefer to talk through ideas before getting a written summary. Let people's preferences guide your choice of method if you want your communication to be accepted, understood and acted upon.

Advantages of the spoken word:

● Provides opportunity for questions, discussion, etc.
● Allows the speaker to assess the effect of their words on the listeners.
● People feel consulted and involved.

- Allows for complicated matters to be talked through and fully explained.
- May be seen as more 'human' and less bureaucratic, by the receivers.

Advantages of the written word:

- Permanent.
- Available for reference.
- Writer can choose words carefully when dealing with complex or sensitive matters.
- Provides evidence of information/instructions/advice given.
- Convenient – can be circulated quickly among many people.
- Minimises overt conflict, personality clashes etc.
- Less expensive than meetings, needs fewer working hours.

It is worthwhile finding out what your people prefer as choice of communication method. We need our communication to be effective, accepted, understood and acted upon; so it needs some effort!

Conclusion

Your effectiveness as a communicator also shows how effective you are as a leader. If people understand you they will work more willingly and effectively with you. More importantly, if you understand your people – do they understand you? You get to know one another through what might be called consultation. Undoubtedly your people will have useful ideas; you need to bring these out, and at the same time build confidence between you by actively listening and, above all, giving credit where it is due. They may know a lot about the running of the business that you do not, and it is vital that you exchange information. What you know you pass on to your people; what they know you also need to know for the effective running of your part of the business. The creation of a harmonious trusting working relationship should be your aim in working with people.

Good communication checklist

Use this checklist to help you think about the way you communicate. It will introduce you to many of the topics that we will cover later on in this book.

Do you:	Yes	No
Plan all significant communications: time, place and content?	☐	☐
Make sure that your message is clear in your own mind before you try to pass it on to others?	☐	☐
Talk or write in language the other person will understand?	☐	☐
Behave as yourself – naturally and relaxed?	☐	☐
Keep to the point – keep yourself from rambling?	☐	☐
Come across as positive, rather than negative?	☐	☐
Put yourself in the recipient's shoes – do you know their needs, interests, motivations?	☐	☐
Keep asking yourself 'Are they interested in what I am saying?'	☐	☐
Illustrate the points – use examples, anecdotes, visual aids?	☐	☐

(Continued)

	Yes	No
Do you:		
Listen to yourself – are you ever patronising?	☐	☐
Avoid mannerisms (these irritate and close people off!)?	☐	☐
Use paper for facts, but speak to people for your reasons?	☐	☐
Get the official story out first and 'beat the grapevine'?	☐	☐
Ask plenty of questions (what, why, who, how, when, where)?	☐	☐
Listen to the answers and the ideas?	☐	☐
Work at listening?	☐	☐
Judge what is said, not the way it is said?	☐	☐
Over-react?	☐	☐
Aim to be flexible?	☐	☐
Resist distractions?	☐	☐
Try to exercise the minds of the people you talk to?	☐	☐
Keep an open mind?	☐	☐

Consider how you use your spare thinking time, during the short intervals of communicating. Do you frame answers, work out quick retorts or put-downs? Think how you react and then think some more about the 'NO' boxes you ticked. Some work to do here?

SUMMARY

In this chapter we have considered the important matter of developing relationships within the work environment, and therefore how to get along with other people. Smooth working relationships enable you to avoid conflict, which is damaging and brings with it ineffective management.

There are several examples of how to deal with difficult people and avoiding defensive barriers on both sides. In getting on with people, common sense, courtesy and good communication are your best companions. Listening to others, asking the right questions and listening to the answers, are really the most productive ways of getting your work done, of getting results.

Don't forget too the written word is as important as the spoken word and more capable of misinterpretation. People take the written word as authoritative – they only have the piece of paper, they haven't the opportunity to ask questions. So, in writing be absolutely precise and clear so that people understand without any doubt or confusion.

03

How do we recruit and select people?

In working with people you will often need to conduct interviews about a variety of matters. Interviewing is a specialised and dynamic form of communication. You will need objectives but must realise that there may not always be a result. This chapter contains some ideas on how to interview effectively, as well as decision making and negotiations.

How to do interviewing

Prepare

The preparation will depend on the type of interview. Some interviews will just happen, and it is not possible to prepare beforehand. Selection interviewing preparation could include these stages:

Preparation for the candidate

Notify the candidate beforehand: give some indication of the probable nature of the discussion. Give them time to think about it.

Location and timing of the interview

Arrange where it is to be. This helps the atmosphere. Formal interviews need a formal setting. Arrange to be uninterrupted. The candidate wants to have your undivided attention. The atmosphere can be destroyed and the impact lost by an interruption at a critical moment. Arrange the timing to suit both yourself and the candidate.

Your preparation

Determine objectives. This will depend on the type of interview. Decide beforehand what you hope to achieve. Research all relevant facts as much as possible. Set your objectives. At first meetings: outline the interview plan. Create rapport and set the candidate at ease. Establish the purpose and objectives of the interview.

- **Establish the facts** The candidate will be able to add more. Give them the opportunity to do so. Open questions are likely to be best at this stage. You are seeking information, probing and clarifying. Concentrate on listening to what is said and noticing what is not said.
- **Analyse the facts** Use reflective questions to analyse the information and evidence gained.
- **Define problem areas** Discuss and clarify. This may produce possible options with useful strategies and tactics. These need to be evaluated against agreed criteria.
- **Reach conclusions and make decisions** Encourage the candidate to talk. It may be helpful to use some closed questions requiring yes/no answers. This will help the candidate clarify thoughts and come to conclusions themselves. Do not try to reach them on their behalf.

- **Formulate plans** These may be targets, courses of action, or development steps based on the conclusions reached. If you have specialist information, provide it at this stage, or suggest where help may be obtained.
- **Summarise** Conclude with a summary of the conclusions and plans and arrange for further discussion.

Other kinds of interviews could usefully be prepared for in a similar way, but make sure that the objectives are clear in your mind before you begin.

Interview skills

In many types of interviews you should encourage the other person to do most of the talking. You need several skills which will be acquired through practice.

Listening skills

A good interviewer:

- listens all the time
- does not divide attention by thinking about their own response when the other person is speaking
- displays good non-verbal behaviour by showing that they are listening
- does not look bored or inattentive.

Questioning and summarising skills

You should control the interview by managing the interchange and asking questions; the other person will have to answer. This can be done loosely by asking open questions such as 'Tell me about …', or more tightly by using closed questions which will probably have 'yes/no' answers. Open questions encourage people to speak, whereas closed questions reduce their opportunity. The type of questions will affect the length of time required for the interview. Interviews and discussions can be categorised as:

- **Seeking clarification** 'As I understand it you ...' 'You feel ...?' 'You think ...?'
- **Summarising** 'So far we have agreed that ... decided that ... etc.'
- **Seeking information/probing** 'How does that affect you?' 'Why do you feel like this?'
- **Suggesting/advising** 'Have you thought of ...?' 'Why don't you ...?'
- **Reflecting back** 'I see, you think you are getting a bad deal.'
- **Agreeing** 'Yes, you're quite right.'
- **Disagreeing** 'You're wrong there.'
- **Criticising** 'You are far too careless.'

The skill is to employ these categories at appropriate times and to realise the effect they may have. Open questions are most likely to be suitable for selection interviews, particularly during the early stages, although closed questions may be necessary to help the candidate clarify their thoughts.

When to remain silent

Many interviewers feel they have to keep the interview going without awkward silences. Used wisely, however, silence can be a powerful way of persuading the other person to open areas of importance that they find difficult to bring out. Some gesture, a slight nod of the head or a smile, and the short silence may provide sufficient encouragement. Too often, an interviewer fails to recognise such an opportunity and may miss the real problem by hastily intervening with some advice or opinion.

'Flagging'

This is a way of indicating the purpose of a remark or question, for example:

'If I understand you correctly, your view is that ...'
'If I may act devil's advocate for a moment ...'

(i.e. I am not actually criticising, just ensuring that we have fully worked out the consequences.)

Experienced interviewers use this technique frequently; it helps to prevent misunderstanding and clarifies the situation. Silence may be one way in which a person 'flags' that a subject is difficult, or that there is 'unfinished business' which might be cleared away by further talking.

Types of interviews

In the course of a manager's career interviews occur frequently. There are different kinds of interviews, for example, selection, appraisal, counselling, and sales but we will only deal with selection interviewing here.

Selection interviews

You will often find that Human Resources (HR) people play a large part in selection interviews. The personnel manager will generally be well qualified to assess personal attributes, take a wider perspective and analyse specific traits. But you should be involved closely with selection because:

- You will be working with the new employee and feel committed to the appointment.
- The prospective employee should of course meet the manager with whom they will be working to see if they like each other. Interviewing is a two-way process.

Preparing for the selection interview

A job description is essential; everyone concerned needs to know that specific requirements are being looked for. The job description should:

- identify the tasks
- examine how, when and why they are to be performed
- identify the main duties and responsibilities
- note the job conditions.

You will probably have some hand in drawing up the job description, nevertheless you should review this and consider the various specifications, as to whether they are 'essential' or 'desirable'. Nobody will score 100 per cent in all areas, therefore you should know, in advance, what are essentials and what can be hoped for, but not necessarily required. Questions should be prepared in advance, to help the flow of conversation and give you confidence.

Personal attributes that we are looking for in the candidate will include:

- personal presentation
- what they have achieved
- general intelligence
- special aptitudes in respect of the job to be filled
- personal interests
- disposition – friendly, standoffish, etc.

- current and past circumstances
- aspirations – what they want to get out of the job.

Managing the interview

The candidate will very likely and understandably be somewhat nervous. Try to set them at ease. You can help by:

- choosing a quiet, private space
- not keeping the candidate waiting
- introducing yourself and others present, and confirming the candidate's name (it does happen that the wrong person is interviewed!)
- explaining how the interview will be conducted
- explaining that you may take notes from time to time to refresh your memory.

Your behaviour throughout the interview will determine its success. These key points should help things go smoothly, but they will need practice.

- Make an easy opening (welcome, something in common, etc.).
- Put them at ease.
- Establish rapport. Build a welcoming atmosphere in which they can talk freely (sensitivity, empathy).
- Listen. Show interest in what they say. Encourage them to do the talking.
- Wait for 'cues' from the candidate. Use them as opportunities to open up sensitive areas or to question further on a topic.
- Note what they do not say.
- Watch for reactions. Silent communication.

- Identify facts. Sift facts from opinions; pick out the relevant ones.
- Look behind the facts. Seek reasons, motivation and explanation.
- Do not prejudge; let the candidate bring out their own personality for you.
- Stay absolutely neutral. Never get into an argument.
- Keep your plan flexible. Be alert for opportunities.
- Keep the conversation flowing. Move smoothly from one subject to another. Change the subject if it has been exhausted or has given rise to embarrassment or is stopping the flow.
- Alter the tempo. This stimulates interest, tests mental flexibility and may reveal a carefully rehearsed performance.
- Use pauses. Carefully used, they can provide the opportunity for the candidate to take the initiative. But 'drying up' will ruin rapport and confidence.

Close the interview firmly and courteously. Give a clear indication to the candidate of what to expect next – a letter, phone call, etc. in a given number of days.

Interviewing is a significant part of the dynamic communication process for which all managers are responsible. Interviewing for recruitment and selection is important for you – after all you are going to have to work with these people; choose well and work will go well. Choose poorly and you could be in trouble.

Decision making

At the end of any interviews for whatever purpose, decisions have to be made. These may be routine, or they may be life or career changing for the people involved. Whatever the decision you come to, it should be structured on the basis of the facts and other information you have gathered during the interview. A satisfactory conclusion to an interview will be a decision to implement the steps agreed. This is a responsibility that any manager takes on and the manager's job is one of constant decision making. Every day we are faced with having to decide on matters either for ourselves directly, or on behalf of others. People are constantly coming to ask 'What shall we do?'. Such problem solving and decision making might be for small things, but we have to take action. The continuous smooth running of our work demands that we do so. There are many sides to effective decision making. An important point is that facts are sometimes not as important as opinions. Dissenting opinions are an essential part of the discussion that leads to good decisions. This also means that you are not entirely alone in the decision-making process; it could – and maybe should – be a team activity. But the final responsibility is yours.

But why should managers encourage dissenting opinions on the decisions they have to make?

- A decision is always a choice among alternatives (one of which is to do nothing). Dissenting opinions are often creative solutions that the manager hadn't thought of.
- A decision is often an instinctive first reaction to something bothering. Testing this reaction against some dissenting opinions can develop a logical solution rather than an instinctive one.
- Sometimes decisions are made on the basis of who is right, rather than what is right. Encourage dissent, but make sure the dissent does not affect the final decision.
- No one is completely without prejudice. Your own opinions often reflect your prejudices but dissent can usually overcome this.
- Many decisions are the right solutions to the wrong problems. Dissent often shows that we have defined the problem incorrectly.

- An effective decision is often a compromise between opposed points of view. To make the best compromise which will work in the long run, let all sides make their best possible case. And remember: facts can usually be found to support any preconceived opinions!
- Good managers will take advantage of their experience of their people in making decisions. People will have opinions based on their experience, but don't have facts to back them up.
- By gathering all these for and against opinions, you can decide what facts are needed to make the best choice of alternatives in the final decision.

A model for decision making

The key factors for any decision in business are:

- Always a choice between alternative courses of action (including the sometimes overlooked one of 'doing nothing').
- Generally a lack of knowledge and uncertainty as to the outcomes of the various alternative actions.

Faced with the problem of choosing between the alternatives in a state of uncertainty, there are three clear steps to follow:

1. **Define objectives** Objectives provide the criteria for the eventual decision. Are the objectives thought through and clearly stated? Conflicts may have to be resolved before agreement on objectives can be reached.
2. **Are there alternative courses of action?** Think through and list any practical alternatives that may be open. Do not ignore the alternative of doing nothing. Define the

courses of action; descriptions should be precise and specific. Try to cover all feasible alternatives.

3. **List the way that things could work out.** Realistic outcomes could be influenced by:
   - general economic conditions which affect the business;
   - total demand for the products or services on offer;
   - how customers might react to the outcome of the decisions.

There are, of course, circumstances that are largely outside the decision maker's control. In listing the alternative outcomes, two points should be watched:

1. Build into the model all significant and relevant outcomes.
   - Keep the total number of likely results to be considered to a minimum; otherwise the complexities of fact gathering and calculation will become unmanageable.
   - What are the chances for each possibility? We need some probability theory here. But the best tool is a bit of common sense! We need to assess, on the available evidence, what is the probability of each of the alternatives discussed actually happening.
2. Calculate the payoff for each combination of action and outcome. These will inevitably be rough guesses or estimates that can be stated in money terms or other measures.
   - State payoffs in terms of the decision-maker's defined objectives. In some cases, negative payoffs may be serious.
   - Multiply each payoff by the probability given to the outcome.
   - Total the results for each action for all possibilities, to get the expected payoff for the action.

All this is going to be time-consuming and will need the active and willing cooperation of your team. At each stage of this process you will need to keep a firm grip on the reality of your situation. You don't have time, or resources, to let this develop into an academic exercise which is not going to give worthwhile results as to what course of action you need to take.

Real problems in a real world

The trouble with techniques for decision making is that people come to believe they cannot make decisions unless they use the right 'technique'. Complex decision techniques are appropriate for major decisions: capital investments, marketing strategy and so on – but the majority of our decisions are not major ones. Often we have few facts and, almost invariably, insufficient time to get any more. So, steer a prudent course between irresponsible off-the-cuff decisions, and trying to get enough information, so that hopefully the answer comes up (correctly?).

No procedure in business is perfect. In solving real problems in a real world the solutions are often compromises, but they are the best available and usually sufficient for the purpose. Another thing about real problems is their indefiniteness. It is rarely possible to get a clear-cut yes or no answer from investigation. Remember you are working with people and things are seldom black and white.

Being inconclusive is a common property of the answers one gets in business. Recognise this fact and make the best of the situation.

Picking where to start

Where does one start on a problem? There is a trick in this. Time to introduce Pareto (see below). There is an important relationship between cause and effect: 'A few causes account for the bulk of the effect' applies to complex situations. This is the Pareto Principle. In collecting data for making decisions, it is never possible to get all the facts; rarely possible to get enough. But it is nearly always possible to be better informed about what is relevant. The right information is usually a matter of quality rather than quantity. Try to pick the right data and interpret it well, instead of hoping that somehow the sheer volume of statistics will automatically provide an answer. Where to start is seldom obvious; the whole job can seem impossibly difficult. We often have to make inspired guesses. It is a step-by-step process that reduces the cost of acquiring data, much of which may be of no value. But remember, most of an answer is usually available from a small amount of information. More data adds knowledge of less and less use.

The Pareto principle

This principle applies to a wide range of human situations. In detail, it states that: 'In any series of events to be controlled, a selected small fraction in terms of number of elements always accounts for a large fraction, in terms of effect'. It is named after an Italian economist who first established the principle in the 1890s.

Here are some examples:

Stocks   20 per cent (say) of all the items in a store account for 80 per cent of the value

Personnel   a small percentage of employees account for most of the problems

Quality   a few of all the possible faults account for most of the rejects

This principle applies very strongly in management as it is really a trick to save work. It has a number of important implications for all managers.

In any situation where there are a number of factors, separate the VITAL FEW from the TRIVIAL MANY.

1. Don't give equal weight to all factors; find the VITAL FEW and give them VIP treatment. This is important for time management also. Concentrate on the vital few, don't waste time on chasing after trivia.
2. When gathering the information needed to solve a problem, note that most of the answers will come from a small amount of information (providing it is the right information on the right key points).
3. The right information is a question of quality rather than quantity.
4. Sheer volume of data rarely provides its own information automatically.

Whenever you are in a situation where you have too much to do in the time available or you are wondering what can safely be delegated to subordinates, REMEMBER PARETO! Find out what is most important and give that your serious attention.

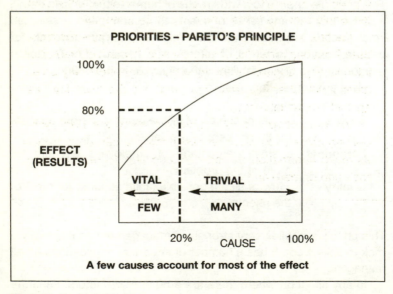

Figure 3.1 The Pareto Principle

SUMMARY

In this chapter we examine several of the essential skills needed for successfully working with people.

Interviewing, of one sort of another, is a key component of the manager's job. It is also a very people oriented activity, and often a one-to-one situation. There are skills in interviewing; you will need to learn how to get the information you need to know; whether you are, for example, recruiting, selecting or conducting a discipline interview. Communication skills are paramount and, above all, listening. You are faced with having to make a decision, the only way you can do that is to be sure you have as many facts as can be obtained in the interview process.

Decision making is a constant in the manager's job. Rarely can a decision be either black or white, right or wrong; it is always a choice amongst alternatives – at best a compromise. However, there are clear steps to follow, but the whole process takes time and can be stressful.

We talk too about the Pareto principle, perhaps the most useful management tool ever devised. It can be helpful in interviewing, decision making, negotiating, and many other managerial jobs, in sorting out what are the 'vital few' as against the 'trivial many'.

We are not all natural negotiators; there are fairly well-defined paths to follow. The best thing you can do is to get as much information as you can (and about the other side too), and prepare and practise.

04

Why plan?

People are the main asset of any business. Its economic success or failure is largely determined by the people that make it up: how well they are managed, how easily their ideas are accepted and how well they are using available technologies. Working with people is a challenge, but the forces at work today give people a greater importance to your business than ever before. As everyone in the business acquires new skills, working with people becomes even more of a challenging task.

Unfortunately a workforce is rarely stable, things happen, changes need to be made. As far as possible, any manager needs to look to the future, do the essential short- and long-term planning and also make contingency plans for things that may never happen – but probably will, and when least expected!

Planning generally

Planning is a primary managerial function and will go on at all levels in the organisation. It is a formal process in which specific objectives are discussed, agreed and set. Detailed ways of accomplishing these objectives are established and many alternatives need to be thought about. There is a prime need to be flexible and:

- anticipate a need to change
- decide what is most likely to change
- be alert to changes in others (and the reasons)
- consider the possible effects on your people.

Planning is usually done at three levels, each having their own emphasis.

- The organisation: has broad objectives in general terms. These will mostly concern the strategic aims of the business decided at board level.
- Functional departments: have sub-objectives and specific detailed plans for their own areas of influence expanded from the overall plans.
- The supervisory level: the sub-objectives here are very specific and the team plans are more detailed and are actually operational plans.

To a large extent plans are based on time; six months is long term for the supervisory level, but short term for the organisation as a whole. Short-term plans will generally be for the lower levels of management. Their operating horizon will be fairly short. Long-term planning (forecasting) is appropriate for senior levels of management who are concerned with the strategic goals of the business.

If management is realistic they plan, because in any business change is inevitable and the organisation must adapt or die. Thus there is a need to plan to cope with change and be flexible to deal with the 'expected unexpected'.

Inevitably changes are certain to affect the economic situation; the organisation may need new policies. Consumer preferences/

fashions/trends may change and there will be a need for new products/services, possibly in new markets. Certainly financial situations will alter and new technologies will be developed. Government legislation changes will involve new codes of practice, possibly new production standards, and environmental conditions or new conditions of service.

All this may be thought out in the planning process, but none can be done without the close involvement of people. The average individual may not notice much change but, sooner or later, how the change affects them is going to have to be explained. This is where your skills in communication are going to be tested – you will have to 'sell' the new ways of doing things. There are various types of plans and, depending on what level you are at in the organisation, you will be participating in preparing some part of them. This is not just a personal involvement; you will need to get members of your team to help in this activity. They will have vital input, by way of data and experience that will be of great value in preparing plans that are realistic and thus likely to work in the situations being covered. Remember though, your plans are but a part (perhaps large, or maybe very small) of the whole. Nevertheless they need to be integrated into the whole picture; therefore the guidelines supplied to you, and that you pass on to your people, should be carefully followed. This means that you:

- set out your objectives
- decide outline procedures
- assign responsibilities;
- explain all this to your people clearly and precisely, plus (and this is very important)
- encourage and answer questions from them.

There are benefits to good planning	and consequences of poor planning
● More effective control ● Greater economies of resources ● Easier delegation ● Better morale	● Lower morale ● Low career prospects ● Lower quality outputs ● Lower job satisfaction ● Higher absenteeism and accidents

Feeling part of the process is excellent motivational practice; your people will appreciate it.

Good planning must have:

- specific goals
- agreement as to how we are to get there
- be attainable and reasonable, and
- be consistent with the overall objectives of the business.

Poor planning happens because:

- there is too little time available
- there are conflicting priorities
- lack of knowledge
- pressures of work.

All these are well-known management factors. When working with people do all you can to get them on your side; your planning will be good, not poor.

Contingency plans

However well thought out, your plans can go astray because of unforeseen circumstances. You therefore need to anticipate problems and set up procedures for coping. No one in normal business can forecast a disaster like a fire, a power cut or plant breakdown. You may be able to forecast a strike (it depends on your negotiating skill), but you need your people to be ready for a possible emergency.

What is needed

Planning is not difficult or costly in relation to the potential benefits. Begin with an assessment of what could go wrong, then determine how to cope with the challenge relating to a potential incident. If an emergency is to be handled successfully, planning should include the preparation of a dossier. This will contain answers to all the likely questions about the organisation. All concerned must know where the dossier is and what it contains. Additionally, you should establish a Crisis Management Team. This group should consist of experienced people, but the precise make-up of the team will depend on the nature of the emergency. However, one member should know about the media. You need to select, train and test your people in realistic exercises. Without this you will not know how key individuals might perform during a real disaster. Some staff will perform very well during exercises and show themselves ready for more responsibility. An important objective in any exercise is to assess how the Crisis Management Team actually manages in the emergency. Training and testing are essential because the company's operational efforts, good or bad, must never be undermined by inept performance caused by ignorance of the techniques required.

We cannot hope to be perfect in our contingency planning, but we can be prepared. We should never allow our team's preparedness to become slack because, if disaster strikes, we are then in real trouble! Maintain the training and testing, it can even be motivational, but at all events, be like a good Boy Scout, be prepared.

Thinking about planning

We know how to plan, most of us do it, consciously or unconsciously. It can get complicated. But by asking ourselves a logical set of questions we can think out a plan clearly. We need some answers, but these steps could get us to where we need to be:

- **What do we want to do?** State the objective. Get clear in your mind exactly what result you want. Write this down.
- **What actions do we need to achieve the objective?** Put down a logical sequence of steps that have to be taken to get where you want to be. There will be gaps, so go carefully and fill them in.
- **Where will we get to?** What will the result be; state this. Try to put some figures on this, more accurate measurement is possible if you do.
- **What will be the benefits from this process?** Try to evaluate the usefulness of this whole process.

When you have done this, sit back and think a bit. The effort has cost you time, but has it saved you time in the long run? Have you been a bit confused as to what you were going to do? Is it clearer now? Does your plan now have a shape to it? The benefits of clear and logical thinking are enormous. Try to plan more often.

Balancing needs and interests

As a manager you need to be very clear about defining team members' roles and your expectations of each person in the role. Trying to balance the competing needs and interests of the person and the job can lead to misunderstandings and poor performance. These misunderstandings may end in conflict. One of the real problems in describing the job is that it is often written as input (what people do) rather than output (what people achieve). When any job is written up in input terms, there is a good chance that there will be overlaps between team members' roles. It is virtually impossible to separate out everything that has to be done. The problem is that people may stick strictly to what is written, and are expected to do so. This often means they become a closed mind. They do not look at the bigger picture – what they need to achieve for the betterment of themselves, their team or the organisation.

Then there is the 'alibi'. In organisations with a rigid hierarchy, input-oriented job descriptions can lead to conflict, as they are often used when something that should have been done, slips through the cracks, for example 'That's not my job.' Even the best written job description cannot cover all situations. Focus on outputs is important because the input terms can lead to a feeling of being overworked. People end up saying 'This is not my responsibility' when they are asked to do something that is not specifically written down. The balancing out of the interests of the organisation with the needs of the individual employee is often difficult to achieve. The business is looking for maximum productivity at minimum cost. The employee needs satisfaction, a feeling of being valued and of having achieved something. If this is at odds with what is written down to do, then reconciliation will be difficult.

You cannot work out the whole range of competing interests and needs by yourself, so it is best to work in collaboration with your team members to gain their commitment. Use the process of writing the job descriptions as a means of reaching agreement between yourself and them, as to what the role should achieve.

Discussing and agreeing output areas with your team members is critical for effective working relationships and getting the results you need. You should not write job descriptions in isolation; nor should they be written by the HR department. Their role should be to coach train and facilitate the writers – the people who will be doing the actual work – you and your team. If a person is going to do the job, they must think through what it is that they are supposed to achieve in that job.

We have to move away from inputs into outputs. An easy way of doing this is to ask 'why?' of each input; then keep asking until the answer becomes an output. Outputs start to repeat themselves, because they focus on the results, and not how the job is done. 'How' is important, but can be stated later when you deal with performance standards and measures. The main thing is identifying the outputs; this will clarify the needs of the individual as against the interests of the organisation. A good by-product of identifying the outputs for each team member is that they provide the basis for results oriented training.

Output-oriented job descriptions for your team members allow you to set the required performance standards. It is vitally important that your team members are involved in this critical element of managing performance. If they are involved from the outset there is far less managing required from you, and they will take more responsibility for achieving the standards they themselves have helped set. Everyone needs to know the extent of their success in achieving the outputs agreed. Ask each team member to list the performance measures and add their list of outputs. Then answer the question: 'How would I know when I am achieving this output?' Answers should include measures that are stated in terms of:

- How many?
- What standard is achieved?
- By when?
- How much?

This self analysis will lead to a process of evaluation to find out how effective they have been.

Evaluate and follow up

The evaluation and follow-up stage is important; it is a thorough review process. This is how we can learn, improve and look objectively at what went well and what went badly. We can then decide on the best course of action to improve performance. In working with people we must not ignore the things that go wrong (and hope nobody notices). Often we blame our lack of success on external factors that we believe to be out of our control. We are working towards a high-performance environment; we have to get rid of negative attitudes from our team. We need to create a reliable review process so as to form a culture where people are ready to admit their mistakes, learn from them, and become better as a result. We have to make time for honest evaluation before moving on. If we don't, then we may end up 'managing frustration'. People have malleable properties; stretch skills and abilities in a particular direction for long enough and they will stay that way for a while then return to their original shape. We often fail to recognise this, and spend valuable time developing new skills in people. But then we don't evaluate and follow up well enough to ensure that the new skill really has become a habit. The important element in evaluation is that if it appears that the individual has not learned from previous development, it should be repeated. You may become frustrated with that member of the team, perhaps even give up on them, feeling they are a lost cause. But quality evaluation and follow-up can avoid people getting stuck in this sort of cycle. To be effective make necessary readjustments to fix the new skills in the right way. Repeat this sufficiently so that, instead of reverting to the previous practice, a new habit is formed. This will need patience and goodwill.

Don't leave anything to chance; adopt a steady approach to developing the right way of doing the job. Stick to the task long enough so that eventually the new method will be secure. Getting the level of ongoing supervision right is a test of our own performance. We have to show a clear understanding of both the topic for development and the individual we are helping. To monitor too closely for long periods of time will be hard work for us and constraining for them. Don't remove supervision too quickly; give an appropriate level of oversight to each individual we are helping. This will ensure that we have enough evaluation time, as well as freedom for them to develop without feeling hemmed in. This instils confidence that we are there to support them, whenever they need our help. Evaluation and follow-up is a fluid and continuous process. We should always be looking for new development opportunities for our people that build on the development objectives that have already been achieved.

Planning checklist

Think critically about your planning. Use this checklist to ensure that your planning process is comprehensive. Tick the Yes/No boxes to get an overall picture of how it is going and what still needs to be done.

	Yes	No
Are my objectives clear for all my critical areas?	☐	☐
Have I plans for each critical area?	☐	☐
Have I thought about my plan far enough ahead?	☐	☐
Have I explored enough alternatives?	☐	☐
Have I collected and used all relevant information?	☐	☐

	Yes	No
Is my plan a commitment?	☐	☐
– or just a forecast?	☐	☐
Am I involving my people in the planning?	☐	☐
Is change involved? If so, is the planning:	☐	☐
– more detailed?	☐	☐
– closely directed?	☐	☐
– more tightly controlled?	☐	☐
Is anything left to chance where a plan is needed?	☐	☐
Is my information sufficient, accurate? or	☐	☐
Am I wasting time collecting and analysing useless facts?	☐	☐
When was my last planning review and update?		

	Yes	No
Am I communicating before, during, after planning?	☐	☐
Am I communicating upwards (for policy guidance)?	☐	☐
– downwards (to the people reporting to me)?	☐	☐
– sideways (to my colleagues)?	☐	☐
Am I planning too early (plans out of date before they start)?	☐	☐
Am I planning too late (leaving no time to organise)?	☐	☐
Is it possible to measure actual results against the plan, using control statements?	☐	☐
If no, is it because:	☐	☐
– plans unclear?	☐	☐
– control information not being produced?	☐	☐
Is it possible to take effective action based on these reports?	☐	☐
Do the plans effectively translate intentions into results?	☐	☐
If no, what do I need to do?		

This last point is the most important. If you have ticked more than half 'NO', then you need some firm action.

SUMMARY

Planning, in its widest sense, is the main topic of this chapter. It is a primary management function in which everyone in the organisation, not just the managers, will be involved. If you do not plan you do not know which way you will be going – no plan, no progress. But even the best of plans go awry, so we need to develop not just one plan, but alternatives. Contingency plans – just in case.

The best plans are those that have involved everyone in their development. They all know what is to happen, what changes are due to come about and how they are going to be dealt with. Planning is not a one-person job; as managers you have to be aware of the teams' roles and to balance individuals' needs and interests. Try to move away from what people do, to what the result of doing will be. We need to evaluate the results of plans, to confirm that they are what was intended. This is a continuous process; it allows for adjustment to plans to bring them back on track if things are not as they should be.

05

How can you support your team?

As you are in charge of other people, you need to organise activity for maximum effectiveness. Here are some ideas for organising the team:

- Allocate the workload equally (or at least fairly). Allow adequate time for high and low work periods.
- The team should endeavour to work in harmony towards the group objective; make sure that people do not pull in opposite directions: try to satisfy conflicting individual and section goals.
- Unforeseen things do happen, so organise for maximum flexibility, to enable the team to cope with and respond to changes.
- The responsibilities, objectives, limits of authority and lines of communication for the team should be very clearly known by the whole team.
- No person should report to more than one manager. Multiple reporting leads to confusion and possible conflict.

Do not allow too many subordinates to report directly to a single manager. (Never more than 15 – and even that's too many!) Again, this could cause confusion.

Don't organise the team around one key individual. Dangerous – what if they are ill, or resign? You will have to regroup; this is time wasting and inefficient. Ensure that as many people as possible know as many other jobs as possible, are efficient in them and are able to easily substitute.

Organising your team

Organisation charts show lines of structural authority and communication, but they will not alter the way people work. They may identify structural weaknesses, but you need to do more than point people in the right direction and see them on their way. Real management means making sure that they continue on the right track; that means planning for what has to be done and controlling the activity. Control comes from monitoring and feedback of information.

Planning

As we saw in Chapter 4 planning starts with an **Intention**, and ends with a **Result**. This is particularly pertinent when it comes to supporting your team.

A definition:

Planning is a process of imagining future events; a synthesis of facts, assumptions and fantasies with the aid of logic, vision and judgement.

Planning in a business context aims to produce practical profitable results. Plan preparation is usually a cooperative effort, and the work of a team to carry out.

Planning objectives

In planning, often too much attention is given to means without the ends being clear. If results are to work out as intended there must be a continuity of planning in between. Generally people will produce the usual results by going through familiar routines without the need for much planning or control. If we want a different (better?) result we need detailed planning, training and tight control.

Setting objectives

To accept accountability for something, people cannot be truly satisfied until they have achieved the things they committed themselves to do; or at least have tried hard. Their self-esteem is enhanced. When working with people you need to get them used to having their results measured; this can worry them. There is a lot of difference between agreeing to a target being possible, and to feeling deeply committed to achieving it. People must feel confident of achieving the results; the opportunity to show success is needed. Guidance in the job is essential until there are mostly successes and few failures. We need to build confidence. You will have to do some personal checking of work; this is the best method of control. But, there is no right amount of checking for everybody. Some people work best with very little oversight, others need a lot, few people need none at all. Make individual assessments and use the right amount for each person.

Some indirect feedback by reports, daily, weekly or monthly is essential. The advantage is that everybody is providing the same sort of information; the disadvantage is that it is remote. But the reports will provide clues as to the different levels of checking needed to ensure that the work is well controlled.

Control systems range from nothing on paper (all done in the head!) to sophisticated computer based controls. For simple cases we can use a checklist as a basis for (some) control. In any event, the cooperation of your people is an essential factor in ensuring that things are on track, so prompt reporting (in whatever form) is needed. In any control system speed and clarity are usually more important than great accuracy. You do not need too much detail when a few prompt simple facts give the same result. The ideal is quick, low cost information sufficiently accurate to guide you to the right decisions.

The importance of planning

Thinking ahead is a must. Unless you do so, actions will often be a series of unrelated, spur-of-the moment decisions and pointless activity. When many events have to relate to each other – they always do in business – planning is essential. The quality of results is determined by the quality of planning. We need to be sure of where objectives start, and where results happen. Broad intentions may be perfectly sound and clearly expressed, but beware of the gaps and wrong assumptions. Gaps in planning are the main cause of wasted business effort.

Decide who should plan, for what, the time frame, and the various management levels. Planning is not an isolated activity; it is interdependent at every level. You can only plan effectively if you are informed of the intentions of your managers; similarly you have to pass on your plans to your subordinates, so that the plans can work efficiently. This continuity implies excellent communications and interpersonal relationships. To make things happen, in the way you intend, it all comes down to people and how you work with them.

Planning involves many people. Unless they really understand and agree with the objectives they may work at cross-purposes. It is worthwhile spending time with your people, planning how planning is to be done. This will save people from solving the wrong problems and avoid wasted effort. It is important that people participate in plans that affect them. Their attitudes can make the difference between plans succeeding and not working properly. To get the best from each individual, find out what their abilities are and make the level of planning appropriate for the people who will carry out the plans.

How to plan

There are many methods of planning, from super formal computerised models to simple back-of-an-envelope stuff. You will evolve your own method to suit your own needs. However, there are some constants that always need to be taken into the planning process:

- Set the objectives, and set the results. The objectives may be specified and outside of your control, so your job is to get the results.
- Check resources available: people, equipment, space, logistics and, above all, the budget.
- Consider the time aspect: when do you start, what are the progress points, when do you have to deliver?
- Use some means of getting all your information down on paper – pattern maps, Gantt charts, critical path diagrams, scatter graphs ... whatever suits you. Bring your people in at this point. Get them to help construct the various charts; the more they get involved, the more they will understand and willingly work towards the required results. If you can't see it all, you can't realistically work out how everything fits together, what comes first, what follows, and so on.

- Once you can see your data, in some form, you are beginning to get a plan.
- Check for feasibility – can this be done, with the resources, in the time?
- Put control points in to ensure that the plan is on track.
- Be ready to adjust the plan as necessary to maintain its viability; or even abandon it if it is no longer functioning. There is nothing more stupid in management than to press on with a plan that is no longer functioning.

You need to think creatively about planning so that it is a comprehensive process. First ask yourself if there are clear objectives for all critical areas, and plans for each of these, with enough thought far enough ahead and with enough alternatives. You need also to ensure that the plan is a commitment, not just a forecast. It is essential to involve your people in the planning, particularly if change is involved. In this case, you should be doing more detailed planning for closer direction and tighter control. Make sure that there are no gaps. Get sufficient and accurate information, but don't waste time collecting and analysing useless facts. It is very important to communicate throughout the process: upwards (for policy guidance) and downwards, so that your people know what is happening. Also sideways to keep your colleagues informed.

Think: are you planning too early (with plans out of date before they start), or too late (leaving no time to organise). Make sure that a measure of actual results against plan is included because, if plans are unclear, little control can be exercised and no effective action can be taken. Plans should translate intentions into results effectively. If they do not, you need to think again so as to get the intended results: this means action on your part.

Introducing coaching

Typically an ideal coach is thought of as someone who advises and shows others how to improve in a particular field. But in working with people effectively we could come up with a much expanded concept which includes someone who:

- Does not give advice, but helps the person find out what they should do. (But does not do the job for them.)
- Is a good listener. (How important this is!)
- Has a calming effect on the person being coached (the learner). (Gives confidence.)
- 'Lives' with the learner's issues, i.e. suspends judgement and really gets involved. (Is empathetic, calm and caring.)
- Displays a positive attitude towards the learner. (Does not hide the realities, is tough when necessary.)
- Is always positive about finding a solution. (The 'we *can* do it' attitude.)
- Is proud of the learner's achievements. (Gets satisfaction.)
- Rarely shows anger or annoyance. (Keeps calm even in a storm.)
- Helps the learner talk things through, particularly when the learner is depressed. (A little talking therapy, sincerely given, helps progress.)
- Provides the learner with a 'comfort zone', where they are free to say what they think and feel. (No discouragement, no sticking to the rules.)

A good slogan for a coach could be:

'Asks questions to help the person find answers.'

Coaching is a development tool you can profitably use with the people in your teams. As a manager, coaching is a key tool for developing your people to their full potential. Coaching encourages the person being coached to take responsibility for their own development. But this does not mean that traditional training is redundant. Rather, it enhances and enables training to be more focused. Sometimes a training course or process can become part of the coaching solution. There will be more about coaching in Chapter 6. To get you thinking about the style in which you could coach, consider the following analysis. This could show you your own management attitude in working with people.

Your coaching style

Coaching successfully is not easy. It is challenging, may be uncomfortable, but gives powerful satisfaction when you see how people can enhance their behaviour and performance because of it.

As in everything in life – and management – there is no one way of doing coaching. What style you practise will be as a result of your own character and preferences. It is unlikely that you will adopt only one style; probably you will find that you combine several. Here are some identifiable styles, with elements that combine to make up the overall style. See if you perceive your own style(s). Tick the boxes in this checklist that best describe you in the coaching role.

Teacher

The traditional role; active and directing and expecting compliance:

- ☐ Have expertise.
- ☐ Good experience.
- ☐ More talking than listening.
- ☐ Collaborative.

☐ Set patterns of imparting knowledge.
☐ Patience.
☐ Clarity of explanation.
☐ Understanding the learning process.

Listener

Acting as a sounding board, and adviser, helping the learner to sort
out their problems themselves:

☐ Providing a 'safe' place.
☐ Empathy.
☐ High level of concentration.
☐ Active listening.
☐ Keen questioning.
☐ Commitment to the person.

Supporter

Provides the enabling back-up to help the learner implement ideas
already thought out:

☐ Listening.
☐ Empathy.
☐ Analytical mindset.
☐ Commitment.
☐ Task focused.
☐ Emotional support.
☐ Equal partnership.

Parent

Something of an authority figure, directing the process rather more
firmly than the Teacher. (It is not wise to use Parent mode too
much; infrequent short bursts where needed to handle immature
learners who may be reluctant to respond to other styles.)

☐ Show firmness.
☐ Directing.
☐ Telling what to do.
☐ Not accepting giving up responsibility by the learner.
☐ Not granting permissions.
☐ Not allowing dependency.

Driver

Very firm, to deal with intractable problems. Shows concern, but straight-talking and focused on what is going wrong and why:

☐ Negotiation.
☐ Questioning directly.
☐ Perseverance.
☐ Clear sightedness.
☐ Commitment to the individual.

You will recognise parts of your own coaching style in all of these. Try to adopt the style(s) that are appropriate in the circumstances – the strategy that is most likely to work. But above all, be sincere and straightforward with your 'pupil'; there is no point in deceiving him, her or yourself, if you want positive results.

Motivation

Motivation is what makes a person do something and put real effort and energy into what they do. Obviously it varies from person to person, depending on the mix of influences on them at any given moment.

A definition of motivation could be:

'Getting people to do willingly and well those things which have to be done.'

Motivation is a high priority in management, however:

- Positive motivation happens when people accept a request.
- Motivation ceases when people are made to surrender to a demand.

Motivation is essential in any job if someone is to give their best to it. If employees are given opportunities for good performance, and have the necessary skills, then their effectiveness depends on their motivation. People are undoubtedly the most important resource; no matter what the degree of sophistication we rise to in our technology, we will still depend on the human factor.

It is your job to motivate your team. You are best placed to create the environment in which people will 'grow' and give their best to their work. However, some factors are usually outside your control or influence: pay, status, terms and conditions of employment and so on. But practical experience has shown that you can provide recognition, responsibility and work that is challenging; all of these have been proved to be among the greatest motivating factors.

The attitudes and behaviour of employees reflect motivation, or the lack of it. Some signs of positive motivation are:

- high performance and good results being regularly achieved
- energy, enthusiasm and determination to succeed
- good cooperation in overcoming problems
- willingness of people to accept responsibility
- willingness to work with necessary change.

On the other hand employees who are de-motivated or who lack motivation show:

- apathy and indifference to the job
- a poor record of time-keeping

- an exaggeration of the effects/difficulties encountered in problems, disputes and grievances
- a lack of cooperation in dealing with problems or difficulties
- strong resistance to change.

Repetitive, monotonous and uninteresting jobs can be made more acceptable if managers recognise the rights of individuals. Many people have had any challenge and interest in their job destroyed by managers' failure to recognise human needs and motivations. It is difficult to state what the most significant elements of the job of working with people are, but motivation must be high on the list. Watch for signs and ignore them at your peril. Watch your own reactions too; if you don't see the signs of de-motivation early enough, your whole work edifice could crumble. It's a tough job being a manager, but with well-motivated people at your side you can achieve great things.

Endeavour to get people to work willingly and well. This increases the individual's satisfaction in their job, and also the organisation's efficiency. Some of the ways in which you can enhance motivation follow.

- Do you:
  - make your people feel valued
  - regularly monitor their work
  - share an interest in whatever is important to them
  - create an atmosphere of approval and cooperation
  - ensure understanding of the importance of their contribution to the team's objectives, and their own function in the organisation.
- Provide scope for development:
  - agree targets for all your people
  - provide on- and off-the-job training
  - arrange any necessary internal and external contacts

- use more skilled people to train others in the specialist skills they may have
- group tasks to use everyones skills to the fullest.
- Recognise achievements:
  - praise and communicate individual successes
  - report regularly to them on the team's progress
  - hold regular meetings to monitor and counsel on an individual's progress towards targets
  - explain the company results and achievements.
- Provide challenge:
  - discuss and agree the team's objectives
  - provide scope for individuals to take greater responsibility
  - fully train at least one deputy
  - encourage ideas and, where practical, allow responsibility to the initiators for implementing them.

Recognition – the vital element

Of all the ways you can motivate your staff, recognition is the most important. People need to feel that they are appreciated for what they are and what they do. The idea of recognition is implicit in all these practical steps and it is a vital management tool that contributes to effective and profitable performance.

Valuing and supporting others

Human relationships exist upwards, sideways and downwards, in business and in all walks of life. Knowing how to establish and maintain relationships is important to everybody; to you, working with people, it is absolutely vital.

The first phase in any relationship is formation; people meet for the first time and get an impression of one another. Impressions tend to form quickly, sometimes based on very slight things. It is important during this phase (and every other one, come to that) to 'be yourself' in a natural, sincere and genuine way.

If everyone does this, then the next phase, consolidation, follows on. The speed of consolidation depends on the mix of personalities and how often and for how long the contact is. This phase could become difficult if the people concerned behave in a non-natural way. You cannot disguise your real self for more than a very short time; it is much better not to try.

The third phase is preservation (or its alternative deterioration). Well-consolidated relationships usually preserve themselves. Others have to be actively preserved. It depends on the strength of the bonds that hold the relationships together; these bonds, in turn, depend on how complementary the personalities of the individuals are.

Things that keep relationships going well are loyalty, integrity, consistency, concern and communication. Things that destroy relationships are: criticism, selfishness, insincerity, indifference, alterations in circumstances or interests and changes in personalities.

Action and reaction

People don't just act according to their own intentions; they also react to the actions or words of others. It is often difficult to judge the true reactions or feelings of other people; at times, we all think one thing and communicate another by words, expressions and body language.

To get on well and value and support other people, control your own reactions and try to predict how other people will respond to what you say and do. There is no magic formula for predicting how people will behave; all are individuals, all are different.

The individual

No two people are alike. Any individual is a complex combination of many factors; in working with people try to understand their make-up. Unexpected reactions may happen because of lack of understanding of a person's make-up. Understanding a person gives you a much better chance of coping with their reactions.

Any individual is made up of (among other things):

- personality, character, temperament
- financial and social position
- domestic situation, health, age
- employment, hobbies and interests, beliefs, academic abilities.

These factors, which are not exhaustive, do not remain static; it is therefore essential to be flexible when dealing with an individual.

Good interpersonal relationships are essential, for workplace success, and for personal happiness. A positive attitude towards life which concentrates on the good things more than on the bad things, and effective interpersonal communication will enhance your value in working with people.

Looking out for other people means:

- seeing things from the other person's point of view (empathy)
- remembering that all individuals are different
- thinking in terms of other people's needs and not just your own.

Do:

- communicate regularly, reliably and clearly with people
- give praise and appreciation where it's due (be careful of flattery!)

- behave naturally and genuinely
- say what you mean and mean what you say
- be loyal to your staff and your organisation
- be courteous to everyone
- admit when you're wrong
- show respect for everyone and express gratitude
- give support when it is needed (but don't overdo it), make sure that people know that you are there for them.

Don't:

- criticise harshly or destructively (and especially not in front of others)
- be tactless or hurt people's feelings
- lose your temper
- show impatience or intolerance
- be unpredictable
- short-circuit lines of communication.

Not surprisingly these 'Dos' and 'Don'ts' are very similar to the rules for good motivation practice, leadership and administration. Management must be treated holistically and although we have to study it one segment at a time, we have to try to encompass the whole in our everyday activity in getting the job done through people.

SUMMARY

This chapter has dealt with team organisation which involves planning, which in turn means thinking clearly and thinking ahead. We have discussed various aspects of planning in an earlier chapter; here we deal with the details of why, when and how to plan, which are fundamental parts of the job of managing. Nowhere is it more important to get your people onside than in the planning process. This chapter also introduced coaching, which will be covered fully in a later chapter.

Motivation is the essence of good management. Your task is to get things done through people; if your team is distracted your plans will not succeed. There are so many aspects to the topic of motivation that it can be said to be the core of the human relations side of the manager's job. One can learn to be a motivator and succeed, or be a demotivator (easy to do without thought!) and not get your job done well or even at all.

06

How do you create learning opportunities?

Coaching, mentoring and motivating are not casual activities and demand thought and attention. The effective manager has a clear understanding of the process, together with a wide range of skills. Providing a genuine learning environment requires a purposeful approach. The manager must know what is to be achieved, and why, and be aware of what they are doing. An effective manager/coach takes any opportunity to help their colleagues to learn.

Coaching

Coaching defined

As we first discussed in Chapter 5 coaching is hard to define. But most people agree that coaching is a one-to-one process, involving direct, two-way communication and discussion.

Coaching is a process in which a manager or, indeed, any person with knowledge and experience, through direct discussion and guided activity, helps a colleague to learn to solve a problem, or to do a task better than would otherwise have been the case. Coaching is concerned with improved task performance, and is central to improving the effectiveness of the organisation. Coaching helps to deliver the goods.

The coaching process

It is unrealistic to break down any coaching process into stages. In practice one bit of coaching merges into another, and into all the other things that go on between the coach and the learner. However, the following are ten identifiable stages in the coaching process.

1. Recognise the opportunity
Coaching opportunities arise from two different sorts of activity: the on-going work routine, and special assignments or job changes.

2. Identify resources
Who can help? Maybe you have the time, skill and involvement to be the ideal person. But often there is someone else in the organisation who could provide assistance more directly, and who has specific expertise.

3. Set the climate
Some of the things that create a good climate for coaching are:
- Set high performance standards.
- Create expectations for personal development.
- Confirm that seeking help is OK.
- Encourage creative risk taking.
- Encourage learning from mistakes.

4. Develop the helping relationship

Many practical and direct activities can be built into the development of the learner.

5. Agree the plan

You need to have a more or less formal meeting. The coach and learner have to establish a shared understanding of who will be responsible for what in the coaching process. This discussion will clarify expectations as to who does what.

6. Set goals and targets

There are two sorts of goals and targets to be considered:
- For the task to be performed;
- For the learning to be achieved.

Agree who should be responsible for initiating and finalising goals and targets. This will vary; the balance of responsibility will be different with work goals than with learning goals.

7. Review how work is progressing

It is important that learners be as open as possible about the difficulties that they are having. Coaches need to use their skills: attending, suspending judgement, and giving feedback. Helping learners to be open about their difficulties. The goals and targets established provide a framework for thoughtful review. Other people involved in the work so far can come in, if the learning climate is sufficiently positive for this to be practicable.

8. Provide help as necessary

The kind of help necessary will depend on the nature of the task that is the focus of the coaching. The style, the timing and the way help is given will vary enormously. There is no 'one size fits all' in coaching.

Provide supportive help early on, in the difficult stages of identifying the problem and generating solutions. At the later stage of presenting the findings, harder criticism may be appropriate.

And at the implementation stage, often the most helpful thing a supervisor can do is to leave the learner to get on without help. The skills of not interfering and suspending judgement are highly important in many coaching situations.

Learners can get stuck with a problem and be reluctant to reveal this. The temptation for the coach is to come up with the solution to the learner's problem. This gives a feeling of competence and hopefully makes the learner grateful. Very often, however, such action does not solve the problem as the learner sees it, and can lead to resentment of the coach. Even if it does not cause resentment, help of this kind can cause dependency. In other words, next time the learner is stuck, rather than thinking things through for themselves, they will go straight to the coach for an instant solution.

The coach can ask a series of questions that give the learner a chance to solve most of the problem themselves. Such questions might be:

- What is the source of your problem?
- Can you identify blocks preventing you from solving the problem?
- Can you work on any of the blocks first?
- Do you need help with working on the blocks?
- How does the problem look now?
- What would things look like if the problem were solved?

By giving chances to review the problem, the coach may help the learner to come up with the solution themselves. If not, more direct suggestions from the coach may be appropriate.

9. Review learning

When the work goals have been reached it is important that supervisor and colleague review the learning goals and targets. In working through them the supervisor should be sure that the colleague has not only thought through the implications of their learning for this occasion, but has also generalised to other situations which they may face in the future.

Bear in mind that no two people will perceive the same situation in the same way. So what a colleague learns will not be what the supervisor would have learned if they had been in the colleague's position. This fact emphasises the importance of asking what the colleague has learned, rather than telling them what they should have learned.

10. Confirm new competence

If someone acquires new competence, the most dispiriting thing that can happen to them is that they do not have a chance to practise it. So, make sure that the learner who has learned how to do something new continues to do it as often as is convenient. This confirms their skill, and fosters their own positive image of themselves, as a learning, developing and growing person.

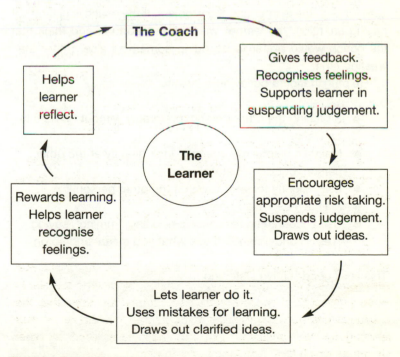

Figure 6.1 The coaching process

Coaching skills

All these skills are part of the armoury of a good communicator and apply not just to your coaching function but throughout your job of working with people. But there are skills that are especially important in coaching. None are particularly associated with any single stage in the coaching process, but all are part of the toolkit of a good coach. Use them as and when needed.

Attending

Pay close attention to the learner. This shows respect, interest and care for both the learner and the problem. If the coach is clearly not paying attention, the learner will feel unimportant, and think that the coach would prefer to be doing something else, rather than wasting time.

Helpful attending behaviours include:

- Sit facing the other person, preferably without barriers in between.
- Maintain helpful eye contact; look directly at the other person, but do not stare.
- Lean slightly forward towards the other person.
- Maintain a relaxed posture.
- Use encouraging responses: nodding, 'mming', saying 'Yes', 'I understand', 'I see what you mean' and so on.

This is all good 'Active Listening'.

Paraphrasing

This is another form of attending behaviour. The listener (the coach) repeats, in their own words, what they think the speaker has just been saying. Paraphrasing enables the listener to check that they are listening to the speaker; both hearing what is being said and being aware of the feelings. It also lets the speaker know that the listener is indeed listening.

Some guidelines for paraphrasing include:

- Listen carefully for the speaker's basic message; watch for non-verbal messages, the tone of voice, and sensing how they are feeling.
- Use your own words when paraphrasing what you think has been said; do not parrot back, nor quote verbatim.
- If you lose the thread of what has been said, or do not understand, say so. If you do not follow the conversation, do not pretend that you do; this could confuse you – and the learner.
- After paraphrasing, look for some sign from the speaker to tell you if your statement was accurate or inaccurate; ask directly, seek confirmation. This reinforces the contact between you.

Recognising and expressing feelings

Faced with a problem, an individual's feelings are involved. These may be anxieties about the problem itself, about some of the other people involved, about their own ability to solve it, and so on.

A skilful coach understands the importance of feelings, and how they may influence behaviour. It is important, therefore, to recognise how the other person is feeling, and be able to communicate your understanding. The first step to being truly comfortable with others' feelings is to be fully in touch with one's own. We express our feelings verbally, but more often we show a great deal in this area non-verbally.

Silence

Many of us do not like silence and it is hard to keep it up. We have the urge to say something, no matter what, in preference to silence. This can be awkward in coaching situations; it can lead to poor reactions and judgements. To maintain silence it is useful to rerun the preceding exchanges over in your mind and keep an open, inviting expression on your face.

Drawing out

It is useful to be able to 'draw out' the learners. This means getting them to talk about problems, feelings and ideas by using questions. Open questions are more effective at drawing out than closed ones that may be answered by a 'yes' or 'no'.

Here are some guidelines for asking drawing-out questions:

- 'What?', 'Why?', 'How do you know?' tend to be open questions.
- If the learner talks only about facts, ask about their feelings.
- If they talk only about feelings, ask about the facts of the situation.
- If they talk in generalities, ask for examples.
- Questions that help to draw out needs and objectives include: 'What do you want to happen?', 'If everything went well, what would it be like?', 'Imagine the problem has been solved – what has happened?', 'What is the worst thing that could happen?', 'What is the best thing that could happen?', 'How would you feel then?', 'What would you do?'.

- Questions that help to draw out ideas include: 'What are all the relevant facts?', 'How do these facts relate to each other?', 'What alternative courses of action are open to us?', 'What will be the likely effect of each of these?'.
- Questions that help draw out assumptions and thought processes include: 'What makes you say that?', 'What happened to make you feel that way?'. 'What if ... (some other assumption)?', 'What other assumptions or conclusions would fit the facts better?'.

Drawing out is a very sensitive process. The coach must take care not to be too intrusive. At the same time, however, we really need to know what is going on, so a light assertiveness is probably best.

Giving and receiving feedback

One of the most difficult aspects of coaching is giving feedback – telling the other person your reactions to them and to their behaviour. Sometimes the coach will be able to tell good things, at other times the feedback will be negative. When giving feedback the idea is to do it in such a way that it is helpful. Often 'feedback' becomes 'slap-back', which will probably have harmful effects on the relationship of both the parties involved.

Here are some guidelines for giving feedback:

- Examine your motives for giving it.
- Feedback should be done at the time of the behaviour in question. Do not postpone it until it is too late.
- Feedback should be given when the learner is ready for it, and at an appropriate time.
- When giving feedback, describe the behaviour concerned, then give your reaction to it.
- Relate feedback to a specific piece of behaviour.

- Give feedback in terms of your reaction to behaviour.
- Ask for reactions to your feedback. Check that it has been understood. Make sure that you understand their feelings about it.
- Give feedback for small specific events. Do not overload.

The coach should also develop the essential skill of receiving feedback. When receiving feedback from another person:

- Listen carefully to their description of your behaviour and their feelings about it.
- Think about it carefully. Try to see the situation from the other person's viewpoint.
- Can you change your behaviour? Discuss this with the other person, and reason out your decision with them.
- You may need help to change your behaviour. They may be able to give you help (possibly by changing some of their own behaviour).

Coaching is a communication process that focuses on learning needs. As part of your (generally unwritten) job description there is a coaching role. This is inevitable; the manager knows the job, the employee may not. As an integral part of working with people you need good performance, so your people have to find out how to do their job well. Coaching is the process of finding out in a structured way and you have a major input into the learning process. Coaching is not teaching, it is learning; the difference in emphasis is important. The responsibility for imparting knowledge is yours, the burden of learning and performing is on the employee. The coach will have done a good job if the learner is able to carry out the tasks or functions acquired through coaching effectively.

There is a good deal of satisfaction in successful coaching; it is time consuming but managers should build coaching time into their time budget. Good results will lead to successful delegation, high motivation, improved productivity and thus profitability. All worth coaching for.

Mentoring

Mentors are fortunate. They enjoy the privilege of learning while helping others to move forward to success. Your mentoring role could be a great boost to your own self-development.

Mentoring is a formal way of helping another person to understand and learn more fully from their day-to-day experiences. It is a protected and confidential relationship where learning and experimentation can occur and potential skills can be measured in terms of competencies gained. The mentor and learner are able to talk freely about any business concerns they may have.

Mentors:

- discuss ideas and explore options with the learner
- support and encourage them
- identify Strengths, Weaknesses, Opportunities and Threats (SWOT) with the learner
- encourage networking and give leads to sources of help
- help develop a plan of action
- advise on the implementation of the plan.

The mentoring process – the 5 Cs

Challenges	What does the learner want to get out of being mentored? What does the mentor want?
Choices	What are the learner's options? How can the mentor best bring these out? What is the learner's best way forward? Can the mentor show the way?

(Continued)

Consequences	What will be the pluses and minuses of both the learner's and the mentor's choices?
Creative solutions	Explore ideas. There should be plenty of mentor input as sounding board and analyst. But the learner should be the driver of ideas.
Conclusions	The mentor guides to work out a suitable plan to achieve the learner's chosen solutions.

Can you be a (good) mentor?

Some people are more suited to the role of mentor than others. The ability to act as a mentor will vary according to the person's own stage of development. For example, someone with limited managerial background may not have enough broad experience to offer. Likewise, someone going through a change in their own business development may lack the mental energy and discipline that the mentoring relationship requires.

Qualities for successful mentors include:

- People with good experiences as learners tend to be good mentors in turn.
- A good reputation.
- Time and mental energy to put into the relationship.
- People competent in the core skills of coaching, counselling, facilitating and networking.

- An interest and willingness to help others, i.e. volunteers are worth more than recruits.
- Willingness and ability to learn and to see the potential benefits.

Key roles of mentoring

Coaching

The mentor, as coach, guides and actively encourages the learner in the development of relevant skills and attitudes for the future. The focus of the coaching role is on the ability to see beyond what *is*, to identify what can *be* and then work with the learner towards achieving that potential.

Analysing mentoring

Mentoring is usefully understood as a special kind of relationship, in which objectivity, credibility, honesty, trustworthiness and confidentiality are critical. But mentoring is simply about regular face-to-face meetings to support a learner in their effort to improve their personal situation or business life.

Mentoring, like coaching, is a process; coaching is an enabling and helping process, however mentoring is a supportive process. It would be useful if the mentoring process was as orderly as the coaching process. Unfortunately this is not the case, but there is a discernable process and, to be effective, it needs to follow a series of logical steps, which are essentially objective setting and confidence building.

Step 1: Discuss learner's own Personal Development Plan, especially any item or area of difficulty. Focus on this and confirm objectives.

Step 2: Encourage the learner's self-management of the problems and the learning route to solve them.

Step 3: Provide continuing support, not uncritical but guiding and giving recognition. This is the crucial phase in the whole mentoring process. The mentor must take care not to become the 'leaning-fount' and be drawn into a 'doing' role. This would be counterproductive for both sides.

Step 4: The mentor should assist the learner in evaluating the process they have gone through together. Agree the measures, e.g.: were the objectives met?; is the learner competent and confident?, etc. The mentor should try to deprecate their own part in this process, not false modesty, but recognising the learner's primary contribution to the process.

The stages in this progression can be outlined as in Figure 6.2, bearing in mind that this is a continuous cycle that can be implemented as needed. However it must be remembered that, whereas a coach is often the direct boss of the learner, a mentor rarely is; in fact it is better if there is no direct relationship.

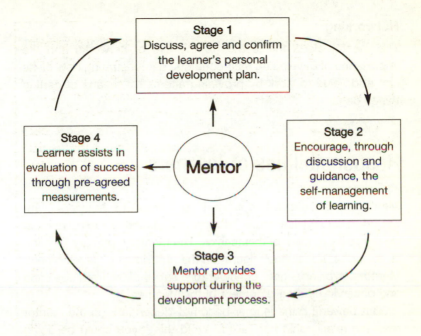

Figure 6.2 The key roles of mentoring

In following these steps to success, you as a manager will also be using best management practice in working with people.

Counselling

The mentor, as counsellor, acts as a sounding board when the learner is solving a problem or making a difficult decision. As a confidant, the mentor helps the learner to clarify the issues involved and to see the larger picture.

Facilitating

The mentor, as facilitator, takes action that indirectly smooths the way for something else to happen. It can be as simple as passing on a phone number or introducing the learner to someone, but it sets in train other interactions enabling the learner to pursue their goals.

Networking

The mentor alerts the learner to the use of networks and the importance of developing their contacts, demonstrating how these can add value to work by providing alternative means of getting things done.

Responsibilities of learners

Mentoring should be confined to providing learners with opportunities, advice, moral support and incentive. Learners must do the rest (i.e. the job) themselves. The mentor's primary function is to be a transitional figure in the individual's development. Mentors, typically, gain considerable satisfaction from assisting and observing the development of their learner.

But beware! If the learner becomes dependent on the mentor then the relationship has failed. Avoid this – you could be doing more harm than good.

Motivation and working with people

What is motivation?

Motivation is the feeling that people have of commitment to doing something well, and being prepared to put energy and effort into it. It varies in nature and intensity from person to person, and on the influences on them at any given moment. These relate to the person's needs, the desire for achievement and the need to feel good about oneself and what one is doing.

Motivation is vital in any job if a person is to give their best to it. Assuming that your people have the opportunity for good performance (correct tools, work method, etc.) and have the necessary skills, then how well they do their work depends on their motivation. Getting people to the place of work ensures attendance. What matters is getting them to work willingly, with effort and effectiveness while they are there.

Signs of motivation

Attitudes and behaviour at work reflect motivation – or lack of it. Motivation indicators are shown for example in:

- high performance/results achieved
- energy, enthusiasm and determination
- cooperation in overcoming problems
- willingness to accept responsibility/accommodate change.

Lack of motivation will be indicated by:

- poor timekeeping/high absenteeism
- apathy and indifference
- exaggeration of disputes/grievances
- uncooperativeness/resistance to change.

It is your job to motivate the team as far as possible. You create the environment in which people will give their best (or their worst!) to their work.

Practical steps in motivation

You need to develop the know-how to get people to work willingly and well, so as to increase the individual's satisfaction in their job and the organisation's efficiency. To do this, practise the following vital concepts:

Make people feel valued

- Regularly monitor the work of your people.
- Share an interest in whatever they hold important.
- Create an atmosphere of approval and cooperation.
- Ensure understanding of the importance of their contribution to the team's objectives, and the function of the organisation.

Provide scope for development

- Set targets by discussion and agreement.
- Provide on- and off-the-job training.
- Arrange any necessary internal and external contacts.
- Use experienced people to train others in the specialist skills they have.
- Group tasks to use everyone's skills to the fullest.

Recognise achievements

- Praise and communicate individual successes.
- Report regularly to them on the team's progress.
- Hold regular meetings to monitor and counsel on an individual's progress towards targets.
- Explain the company results and achievements.

Provide challenge

- Agree and communicate the team's objectives.
- Provide scope for individuals to take greater responsibility.
- Fully train at least one deputy.
- Encourage ideas and, where practical, allow people to take responsibility for implementing them.

Recognition – the vital element

Of all the ways that you can motivate staff, recognition is the most important. People need to feel that they are appreciated for what they are and what they do. The idea of recognition is implicit in all these practical steps and it is a vital management tool which contributes to effective and profitable performance.

'Well-managed people are well-motivated people.
Well-motivated people are happy people.
Happy people work well and are productive.
Productive people make profits.'

Lord Sieff

Of all the motivation theories that have been promoted over the years (see Figure 6.3), Herzberg's satisfaction and dissatisfaction (motivation and hygiene factors) theory seems to be the most relevant and practical in our daily working lives, especially in relation to the idea of recognition. Frederick Herzberg asked many people in different jobs at different levels two questions:

- What factors lead you to experience extreme dissatisfaction with your job?
- What factors lead you to experience extreme satisfaction with your job?

He identified a number of factors that lead to job satisfaction and job dissatisfaction. The collated answers show the order and frequency in which the factors appeared.

Potential satisfiers (motivators)	Potential dissatisfiers (hygiene factors)
Achievement	Company policy and administration
Recognition	Supervision
Work itself	Interpersonal relations
Responsibility	Work conditions
Advancement	Salary
Growth	Security
Job satisfaction (motivators)	**Job dissatisfaction (demotivators)**

Figure 6.3 Herzberg's motivators and hygiene factors

Dissatisfaction (hygiene factors)

The factors on the right side of the chart tend to cause dissatisfaction rather than satisfaction. Further investigation showed that the dissatisfaction was only present where the factor (e.g. salary) was not fulfilling the expectation of the employee. If the factor was changed to the employee's expectation, it merely disappeared as a source of unhappiness. It did not create satisfaction. Another important point to note in these factors is that they are all concerned with what is done to or for an employee, or is concerned with relationships over which they do not have full control.

Satisfaction (motivators)

Factors on the left side of the chart have little to do with money and status. They have much to do with achievement and responsibility.

They are connected with the job content, i.e. the things that people do at work. These factors were identified as providing greatest satisfaction at work.

The moral for you and for working with people is clear; pay particular attention to the types of tasks people are expected to do. Job satisfaction comes from our involvement in doing what we think is worthwhile and challenging.

Ways to effectively demotivate

Unfortunately there are more ways to demotivate people than to motivate them. Sometimes it is our unconscious or thoughtless words or actions that put people off. It is only too easy to do some of the things listed below. So if you, as an individual needing to get things done through people, find yourself doing any (or all!) of these things – **stop!**

- Don't take them into your confidence, keep them in the dark about the real purpose of their work.
- Make sure you get credit while they get the blame.
- Never admit that you might be wrong.
- Don't give them sincere praise.
- Put them on work for which they are temperamentally unsuited.
- Let them get involved in a really serious mistake before you pull them up.
- Talk about 'objectives'; that is, the results required, but make it quite clear that not rocking the boat and conforming to the system is really much more important.
- If they come to you for real help, give them platitudes.
- Harp on details while ignoring the real issues.
- Avoid giving advance information about changes that affect them.
- Discourage new ideas.
- Insist that they do the job your way.

- Make it clear that it never pays to step out of line.
- Demonstrate that promotion goes to those who ingratiate themselves rather than those who perform.

Every one of these actions is a **cardinal sin of management**. If you really want demotivated staff, go ahead, practise these boorish actions. If you, on the other hand, want well-motivated, productive staff, avoid these actions like the plague.

Create the right climate

In order to motivate successfully, you have to be able to recognise basic human needs and to be aware of the process of motivation. It is useless to make a spasmodic approach to motivation: it is a continuing task of management and the first rule is to establish the right climate. To create this:

- encourage a sense of the importance of the job
- develop a sense of involvement amongst your people
- give evidence of management efficiency
- display evidence of management openness
- create a sense of teamwork and team identity.

Respect people as individuals; get to know what motivates each one. This must be on a continual basis; when motivation is the issue you are always on duty.

Motivating people

How do you motivate your people? Think about these items individually, then arrange the characteristics in the rank order (1 = high and 8 = low) you think is best.

Factor	Rank	Definition
High pay		Paying them a salary that will enable them to improve their standard of living.
Advancement		Giving them the opportunity to learn new skills or be promoted to more demanding jobs.
Pleasant companions		Working with people who are friendly and approachable.
Autonomy		Allowing them to set their own objectives (within your framework), to plan their day, and to have control over how they do their job.
Security		Providing an assurance of continued employment and a comfortable retirement.
Responsibility		Delegating decision-making and holding them accountable for results, including the control of resources.
Status		Recognising the importance of their position in some non-monetary but tangible way.
Achievement		Giving them the opportunity to solve problems and see the results of their efforts.

Thoughts about these motivation elements

Most theories of motivation agree on a general order of importance for these motivation factors. Some of the factors will not be controllable by yourself; for some you can have a significant input. This analysis and ranking (from high to low) is based on Herzberg's Motivators and Hygiene Factors. This theory (it works!) is very appropriate for working with people.

- **Achievement (1)** You can have a major input into this. You can create opportunities for people to actually achieve something important to themselves, to the team, to the job. The feeling of self-worth from this is enormous.
- **Advancement, Autonomy and Responsibility (=2)** Again you can have a major input into these factors. Certainly you can recommend promotion if the person has performed consistently well. Also you have control of working arrangements, which means that the levels of responsibility and autonomy can be arranged so as to give the individual the satisfaction of doing a job with little or no supervision, and producing a good result. Although these are distinct characteristics, it is very difficult to disentangle them; they work together with each forming part of the other.
- **Pleasant companions (5)** This is a low level motivator and indeed is one of the factors that can cause a lot of dissatisfaction. It is one of the things that you, the manager, can influence. If poor relationships are seen within the team, then step in and help sort things out.
- **High pay (6)** Again, this is a low level motivator and you will generally have little or no influence on pay rates. Pay is never sufficient, and although raises are welcome any incentive effect soon wears off.

- **Security and Status (=7)** Surprisingly security and status figure very little as motivational factors. Security is mostly a contractual matter which we accept when entering the job, although in times of economic uncertainty it may well rise higher up the scale. Status in a work situation rises with promotion; again we accept our position in the scheme of things. It is rare that status matters very much to people. However, respect and recognition do matter, but these should not be confused with a person's status or position, high or low, in the organisation.

To motivate your people effectively, use the tools that you have some measure of control over. Organise tasks so that people get a sense of achievement from doing them; try to keep your supervision light and give plenty of sincere recognition.

SUMMARY

This chapter has dealt with some of the critical elements in your job of working with people. The manager is, in some respects, a trainer; this does not mean that you have to get people into formal classroom situations and teach them, but you do need to back them. But people often need to be shown how to do things – by means of demonstrating, correcting and monitoring, helping them to do their work satisfactorily. You are the person who knows how to do the job, it is your task to ensure that others can do the job well too.

Mentoring is closely related to but must not be equated with coaching. In fact a mentor may not know how to do the job at all. The role of the mentor is to encourage, act as a sounding board, listen and try to help the individual sort out their own problems, not solve them. It is a difficult but rewarding role and generally a greatly appreciated one.

(Continued)

Motivation is an essential part of the manager's job. If your people are in a demotivated state, the work will get done poorly, if at all. You need well-motivated teams to ensure good performance. A serious measure of your success in working with people is the level of their motivation: high means that your work will get done well; low means that you may not survive.

07

How can you help people to develop?

We all develop our own personal ideas about the meaning of work; what matters to us in doing it. Changes in the things that make people want to work mean that the organisation must be:

- flexible to accommodate individuals' needs
- open in communication with employees and all those with an interest in the performance of the organisation
- accountable, and
- open to change, especially the need for continual training in new skills.

Managers need the skill to identify and promote the factors that motivate their team. People expect work to give them a measure of self-expression, for example, that doing work they feel to be worthwhile, personally satisfying, or feeling that they are making a contribution. People will take on responsibility for their actions, but they expect the company to be accountable, i.e. what is its success in the market? in holding and developing people? and how well is this reported? The organisation has the responsibility to communicate information about its own performance in the market to its employees. This provides support to people; if they know how 'their' company is doing, they feel secure. People want new skills, not necessarily for power or status. The manager's job is to identify new career development opportunities. Development of people should include, not only technical training, but also personal and managerial development. People are keen to develop their own personal skills; this is both motivating for them and also maintains their value to the organisation. However, if you are not sensitive to what motivates people, they may look for satisfaction elsewhere. You need to stimulate employees to give enthusiasm and commitment to work. If people enjoy what they do at work, they will get more out of it and put more into it.

A little learning theory

There is something about the mechanistic approach to learning that deters managers and workers from developing an enthusiasm for it. People are more likely to learn when they want to learn. People learn when they are competing with others for recognition and praise, or when they see that they can apply their new skills in order to contribute to the results of the organisation. They learn when they realise that new abilities help them progress. Effective people development has great beneficial effects for the organisation. It eases many problems: high staff turnover; poor human relations; lack of engagement.

Learning opportunities and development

First of all, what is learning in a work context? It is:

- acquiring or developing new knowledge or skills
- increasing competence to deal with the work environment
- changing our attitudes and behaviour to try to improve performance.

Learning opportunities will come up in surprising ways. What we have to do is be aware of the possibility. But what are we looking for? Do we want our people to:

- show more initiative?
- be more creative?
- confront their problems and not expect us to solve them for them?
- question what is happening, because they want to do things right?

People can learn:

- if they have the ability to do so
- if the system allows or encourages them
- if they are forced or coerced to; or, and most importantly,
- if they want to.

It is a vital part of our job to somehow make people want to learn, to enthuse them with the ideas of change and self improvement. People will usually have had a lot of experience and will have learned from it. But they also will have set habits. They are proud and like to see themselves as independent. Inevitably they will have things to lose and will not like choice or ambiguity. They will naturally have preoccupations other than learning, but this can change given the right incentives. Nevertheless they may find it hard to change. Everyone has something to contribute, but there is still the fear of 'going back to school', coupled with a deep fear of falling behind or losing their job if they don't join in.

People can change if they have the ability, but sometimes are so fixed in their ways that it is very difficult for them. The system needs to encourage them because, when working with people, we can't really force or coerce them to change. So they learn if they want to and if they see the relevance and value of what they are learning. They also need to know what goals are set and they must be doing something to which they can relate. Past experience is very important; what they are now being asked to learn must somehow be familiar. Something completely strange is likely to be rejected or ignored. People need to be comfortable with what they are learning. Your job is to create an atmosphere of openness and confidentiality. People appreciate that, particularly if they are struggling with new ideas or methods. When people are aware of their problems, encourage them to ask questions. Then they will become aware of different interpretations of situations. This will encourage exploration of ideas and encourage people to think around the subject. Above all get people actively doing things.

Encourage your people to grab every learning opportunity that comes up. Good open communication with them can turn what might be a dull instruction session into something enlightening to which they feel they have contributed. Learning is motivational and can be fun.

But what sort of learning or training do your people need? You will probably be able to see where certain parts of your operation are not performing as well as planned. You may be able, by observation, to identify either the system, or perhaps certain of your people, who are not up to scratch. You could try having quiet words with such people to see what their problems may be. You do not have to go on to a full-blown training needs analysis, when some appropriate coaching is really all that is needed. The feedback you get from the learner and their coach will show you whether this informal approach is working. If it is not getting the results expected, then a more formal training route may have to be considered. Each individual will have different training needs, or indeed will want to learn different things. Your job as manager is to facilitate the learning requirements for your work and also satisfy, as far as possible, the learning aspirations of your people. To maintain the standards of performance for your responsibility area well-skilled people are essential. Your job as manager is to ensure that those skills are available and well used.

Perception and empathy

Our perception of other people is formed by our needs; we distort the world in relation to our tensions, e.g. are these people friends, or are they a danger? Wishes and fears are both important to our needs. We set goals towards achieving what we want, and to avoid what we dislike or fear. We see in other people what we want to see and also what we may be afraid to see; our perception is selective. What we select to perceive is based on three factors:

- seeing what promises to help satisfy our needs
- ignoring mildly unpleasant ideas
- paying attention to things that are really dangerous.

These factors influence our feelings of empathy towards others. Our perceptions guide us in our assessments of people. We all have some relatively unchanging characteristics; our perceptions are perhaps instinctive reactions, either to physical appearance, or some deeper psychological matter. Our information about a person is collected from our perception about their 'personality' or ways of behaving. We might ask ourselves some questions:

- How do they see other people – friends or enemies?
- How do they get on with superiors and subordinates?
- What sort of attitudes do they adopt?
  - enthusiastic?
  - cynical?
- Do they conform or not?
- How do they control moods?
- Are their methods consistent or variable?

The answers to this kind of question will be hard to find, but asking them will give you some sort of guidelines about the personality of the individual you are dealing with. But, having made your assessment, you can now consider what the best way will be of communicating, so as to develop a good relationship.

Relationships, influencing and inspiring

People behave in certain ways to satisfy their needs. In satisfying those needs they depend on other people. At the same time, those people will also be dependent to satisfy some of their needs. An influencing relationship will be formed. Relationships can be defined as 'situations in which individuals or groups seek mutually to inspire and satisfy needs'. Dependency in a relationship is usually two-way. For example: an employee depends on their employer for the job. At the same time the employer depends on the employee to do the work, maintain standards and develop the business to satisfy the 'needs' of the company.

As managers working with people, we need to find a realistic meeting place, because people always do what they feel to be the most appropriate thing for them to do at the moment of action. So we should always look at the situation through the other person's eyes and be empathetic. Try getting feedback to discover and understand why people behave the way they do, rather than passing judgement or blaming them for their behaviour. Ask 'Why do they think they are right?' rather than 'How shall I put them right?'. Talk to people; get them to feel more capable, more necessary and more useful. Never demonstrate your own superiority. Look up with them, do not look down on people. Look at your own behaviour critically, and get some feedback which will help you learn to live with people rather than try to change them. Change their working environment in such a way that they can 'see' and evaluate their efforts more clearly, and so come to change themselves of their own accord. Every day presents a learning opportunity and, by inspiring your people with the need for change, they will accept the advantage offered by the open and empathetic environment that you create. Work will go more smoothly, problems will be solved swiftly and productivity will greatly improve.

Getting and giving feedback

The idea of feedback is to learn as much as possible about how people are doing in their job (and that, incidentally, includes you). If you find out that something is going wrong, it can be corrected. If it is going right, you can give it a bit of praise. But in the end it is about how much openness and honesty that develops within the group that affects performance. This involves getting and giving 'feedback'; information (both positive and negative) that is useful and helpful to others.

The first step is to establish trust. There are always times when people find it difficult to have their proposals and even their actions rejected. To gain trust, show your people that you respect them, and keep your comments to a professional evaluation of their work. Then it is essential to accurately assess the individual's readiness to accept negative personal feedback. Wait until the person either seeks advice or asks for some help. When pointing out a shortcoming, be non-judgemental but be specific. Detail particular actions, behaviour, or incidents, and the impact that resulted from these, on the person themselves or on others. Finally, check for understanding, because without clear understanding the feedback recipient may be either confused or defensive. The purpose of feedback is to be helpful, so that something can be done with it; to change some behaviour or to be more aware of their impact on others.

You may ask if the person understands what you are saying, or if they need more specific examples or added information. Also ask them to get comments from others to see if they feel the same way. What you are trying to do is help the recipient overcome any confusion, anger or resentment.

Receiving feedback

Often we block others from telling us their feelings; we fear that we may be hurt or insulted. This might be appropriate and useful at certain times but often denies us useful information. When we receive feedback the usual sequence is: first: anger or resentment; second: confusion, and then finally: acceptance or understanding. We often confuse our intentions with other people's feelings and their perceptions of us.

We may intend to present our ideas clearly but perhaps they are seen by others as not well thought out or lacking support. Often when we find resistance to our ideas we withdraw and stop participating. We feel that what we intended is not what is perceived by others. When working with people learn to expect this sort of sulky disappointment. Advise the people you work with to ask those they trust for help or advice. Specifically, ask how others felt or what reaction they had. Get specific examples and then they can clarify their perceptions. Finally, when receiving feedback you need to make a decision either to accept it and take some corrective action, or reject it. Often some information will not be factual. You must differentiate between help that we ask for from those we trust, and incorrect perception by others that is not useful.

Ideas on feedback – some bad, some better

Here are some extracts from actual feedback sessions with a commentary on them. Some of the remarks are downright rude; others are placatory and may hit the right spot. In giving feedback to your people, always try to find the meeting point where your perceptions meet the reality of the person.

Remarks	Commentary
I don't know what it is about you, but to be honest with you I think you create antagonism among your subordinates. I can't tell you why I feel this way, I just do!	Your intentions of honesty will not automatically cause trust and openness. Specific examples do more to help individuals evaluate their behaviour.
You simply don't understand; that wasn't what I intended at all.	There is a difference between our intentions and how our behaviour is perceived. Although you may intend one thing, your behaviours are what is judged. It's important for you to have an understanding of how someone else felt. *(Continued)*

Remarks	Commentary
I am what I am, and I have a right to that. No group of workers has the right to dictate to me what I should be like.	You certainly have the right to be who you are and to be what you want to be. However, if you want more understanding of how others see you, or if you want to change some of your behaviour, it is wise to ask others what they like and don't like about the way you behave.
You may not want to hear this, but for your own good you should know that several of your colleagues feel you are lazy.	The first rule of feedback is that it is meant to be helpful and best given only when another person openly asks for help or advice. Specific feedback can build trust and understanding.
Thanks for your help; no one has told me that before and I find it hard to believe that I'm seen that way. Could you give me anything more specific? I'll just have to get some thoughts and comments. No one's perfect, you know.	This is a perfectly good way to deal with feedback that you don't quite understand. By not criticising, you are maintaining a good relationship while still being able to get more information that you need.

SUMMARY

In this chapter we have considered several important aspects of working with people.

Firstly, we saw that what matters at work are the ideas that you need to share with your people about their own responsibility for self development, and your ability to motivate them to that course of action. We then discussed a little learning theory and the benefits to both the individual and the company of the learning process, whereby enhanced understanding and ability will be very productive; this includes an analysis of how and why people learn and the benefits that this experience brings.

Understanding our perceptions and the ability to be empathetic are essential elements for success in working with people, as is competence in giving and getting feedback.

This chapter is a valuable addition to developing your general communication skills for successful managing.

08

How can you deal with conflict and problems and build a team?

One of the most important activities in which a manager is involved is problem solving. Problems, of whatever nature, arise; the manager will generally be the closest to them, knowing the background and the underlying causes. Problem identification, and analysis of the symptoms that are occurring, become the manager's responsibility. This is an inevitable task but, if problems are holding up the workflow, then the manager cannot achieve the main objective of the job – to get things done. Problems need to be solved in the most rational, time- and cost-effective way possible.

Solving problems

Tackle the problem-solving task in a logical way. First do an initial analysis of the background to the problem. We need an understanding of what the problem is about; this puts us on the track of a reasonable solution. We can then identify the real problem, which symptoms conceal. We can deal with the symptoms but sooner or later the problem will come up again; so it is vital to identify what the problem really is.

If we are satisfied with the real cause, we can attempt a solution to the problem, using various techniques. Something that is often forgotten in the problem-solving process is the final stage. This is evaluating to see if the solution is working, then monitoring to ensure that it continues to work well.

All this is time consuming and is a heavy responsibility for the manager, but it is an essential part of the job. A good problem-solving manager gets things done without too much fuss!

How to define and handle problems – a six-stage process

The following is an outline of a process that can be helpful in standing back from what might seem to be an intractable problem, and being able to get some clarity. Using this framework is a good way to get your team working together

1. Define the problem

There are two kinds of problems: 'what' problems that require you to determine the precise cause, and 'how' problems. These focus on how you are going to solve the problem, when the cause is known. It may be better to deal with most probems as 'what', until you are absolutely certain of the cause. We often tackle the symptoms of a problem rather than the real issue, because we assume we know the cause when in fact we don't. The real problem is not always apparent. For instance, complaints about salaries often conceal a real problem, such as a boring job. To get at the 'what' examine all the possible components: is it the people, is there an individual who is making trouble, is it a group who are dissatisfied with their conditions, are there delivery or production hold-ups and so on? The reasons are many: your job is to pinpoint the cause, which leads you into stage 2.

2. Gather the information

Gather everything: at this stage do not differentiate between facts and opinions but categorise them. Then, interpret the information; sort out facts from opinions; select information that is relevant to the problem. At this point you may realise that you have defined the wrong problem! This realisation is the true value of this process. Go back to Step One and start again.

3. Develop solutions

Develop several solutions. Don't worry at this stage about how feasible a solution Is. This is a sort of focused brainstorming; you want many solutions, from which you can choose the best.

4. Select the best practical solution

Note the word 'practical'. If you can, pre-test your better solutions to identify the best. Run small pilot tests. In the end this can save you considerable time and money. Otherwise, you may have to analyse each of your solutions to determine which has the highest chance of succeeding; go with that and make changes and corrections as needed.

In theory, one solution might be ideal but not economically practical at this stage. For example, if the office is overheating, a move to an air-conditioned building might be the ideal solution; a more practical one is to install fans.

5. Put the solution into operation

Now try your best practical solution. Plan its introduction; carefully decide what needs to be done, write down the action steps needed, then begin. If working as a team, and parts of the work can be delegated, do so.

6. Evaluate and monitor the effectiveness of the solution

An important stage, which is frequently forgotten. Make sure your solution is working. Have a contingency plan. This will help successful resolution of problems that may happen later on. If problems do arise, solve them by going through this six-step process again.

Problem-solving ideas

Here are examples of a wide range of problem-solving ideas, hints and tips that you can put into operation and get good results. As we are working with people, these are primarily dealing with people-centred problems; technical matters can often be solved with a twist of a spanner, or a bang with a hammer. People, however, need gentler, more subtle treatment!

Dealing with difficult people

These tactics may help you cope with people who are difficult to deal with:

- Kill with kindness. Treat everyone well, no matter how people treat you. Be direct – but likeable and polite. Don't treat a thoughtful person thoughtlessly.
- Listen, don't interrupt, then respond. Allow the difficult person to express their feelings fully. Show that you are aware of the situation, describe what you see and hear, reveal what you think and feel, say what you want.
  Tip: Don't judge ('You shouldn't be that way') or generalise ('You always do that').

- Don't take a position – deal with a need. Find out what motivates the person, so that you can offer alternative ways of solving the problem. It is probable that the difficult person confronting you has simply adopted the most obvious solution. Move from what the person wants to why they will want it.

- Accept blame. More often than not, you will have played some part in bringing about the behaviour that others subject you to. Admit your fault quickly and emphatically. Whenever you shoulder your share of the blame, others are more likely to own up to theirs.

  Tip: Sometimes you can encourage the other person to cooperate by claiming more responsibility than you deserve, 'Yes, that's probably my fault' (even if it isn't).

Settling disagreements

You may get into arguments where you and another person have developed rigid viewpoints. Your comments to each other become increasingly bitter until all progress stops. In most cases the basic problem is a breakdown in communication.

Tip: Try to stop the argument. Ask the other person if they will agree to a new ground rule for both of you: neither will be allowed to speak up or to state their side of the argument until each has stated the opponent's ideas and attitudes to the other's complete satisfaction. In this way you are forced to think like your opponent and see their point of view.

Crisis and bad-news guidelines

Make sure your staff know how and when to let you know if things go wrong. Make it absolutely clear that you will NOT shoot the messenger. Offer them these guidelines:

- Report the problem promptly. 'Tell me right away'; this will allow you to solve the problem before it gets worse.
- Give me only the necessary facts. Don't overstate the problem, this could make it look worse than it is. Think it through before you report and be ready to explain exactly what happened.
- Use tact. Don't say something like 'This is a terrible situation'. Instead say 'Here's something I thought you should know about'.
- Offer a solution. Don't just tell me we've got a problem. Recommend a way to correct a mistake or an error in judgement, and explain how you'll prevent it from happening again. Try saying 'Don't bring me problems, bring me answers'. Encourage your people to think about and present their own solutions – and give these serious consideration.
- Don't deliver only bad news. Pass along the good news also. That way, when you do have bad news, I'll take it better and your suggestions for improvement will have more impact.

How to make difficult decisions

In working with people you will often have to make difficult decisions; here are some suggestions for dealing with them, but you will need to prioritise the urgency of the decision to be made. You may not have the luxury of thinking time, so a clear head and good background information are essential.

- Accept that you can't control the outcome of a decision. All you may be able to do is influence the decision-making process.

- Identify your needs and wants. Put them down on paper – even if they are contradictory. Writing things down often highlights a logical pattern in a problem.
- Rank the things you want and need. If you spot contradictory needs, ask yourself 'Which would I choose?'
- Gather all the information necessary to make the decision. Look at alternatives, consequences, advantages and disadvantages. Do not let your emotions interfere with this process. Be as objective as possible.
- Determine how much of a risk you are willing to take. Consider these strategies:
  - Choose the safest alternative – one that can't fail.
  - Pick the option with the best odds for success.
  - Select the alternative with the most desirable outcome, despite the risk.
- Cut out any option that might present a loss you will not be able to accept – despite high odds for its success.
- Think about how you would deal with negative consequences.

Acting assertively and decisively

To be effective at problem solving you need a certain level of assertiveness. There are basically three behaviour styles: being passive, being aggressive, and being assertive. You need to be conscious of which style you present to others because there are difficulties with each.

Assertive behaviour is getting things done without damaging others; acting on what you think is right without denying the rights of other people.

There are several kinds of assertive behaviour:

- Simple assertion: 'I would like this.'
- Empathetic assertion: 'I see where you are, but I need this right away.'
- Confrontative assertion: 'I understood that you would do this and you haven't.'
- Angry assertion: 'I feel very angry about this, I would like you to do that.'
- Soft assertion: 'I appreciate that you did that, it made me feel good.'
- Persuasive assertion: 'I appreciate your problems and wondered if you would do this.'

Use whichever gets you the best results.

Assertiveness difficulties lead to inadequate behaviour. If you are non-assertive or passive, you seem to be weak. Because you do not stand up for yourself, you feel hurt, anxious and unsure. Your weak actions and reactions may set you up for ridicule by others.

If you behave aggressively you may seem too strong. You may feel you want to hurt others, because you perceive a need to defend yourself. Aggressive behaviour may accomplish your ends temporarily. But in most cases it leads to disrupted communication, brings out counter-aggression from others, and tends to make you even more aggressive. This is a descending angry spiral.

Properly assertive behaviour does not always result in the accomplishment of your goals. But it does lead to a good feeling about yourself. When things don't work out, you may feel disappointed, but you will not feel irrationally hostile.

The following table summarises these three attitudes.

Table 7.1 Levels of assertiveness

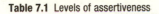

Assertion vs. Aggression		
Difficulties lead to INADEQUATE BEHAVIOUR		
Non-assertive ● you feel ● others feel	**Too weak** hurt, anxious and unsure scornful of you	**LOSE/LOSE**
Aggressive ● you feel ● others feel ● long-term loss	**Too strong** vindictive, defensive, short-term gain resentment, hostility and angry reaction	**WIN/LOSE**
Assertive ● you feel ● others feel	**fair** good about yourself, even if you do not achieve short-term goals. possibly disappointed, but not irrationally hostile. respect, concern, involvement, long-term win	**WIN/WIN**

Here are some techniques that will help you to get things done:

Be authentic

- Tell others what you want.
- Receive and give 'positive' comments.
- Take care of your needs. Evaluate and seek clarification of requests that you receive.
- Confront problem situations quickly.
- Do not assume.

Work within your abilities

- Do not exaggerate your strengths and weaknesses.
- Do not act helpless if you can act independently.

Language

- Use 'I' statements – avoid 'we' and 'you' – simple statements, brief and to the point, silence – until you know what you want.
- Do not use unnecessary statements or over explain or answer manipulative questions. (Question, reflect on or summarise questions.)
- Know when to leave it alone.
- Do not criticise those who do not need or want your help or help those who do not need or want your help.

You are working with people, and people, as we know, are sometimes difficult. As you need to get decisions made and get things done, a little appropriate assertiveness is needed. The table below outlines the characteristics commonly found in the three attitudes of interpersonal behaviour.

Table 7.2 Interpersonal behaviour

Passive	Assertive	Aggressive
too little too late too little never	enough of the appropriate behaviour at the right time	too much too soon too much too late

Effects*	Effects*	Effects*
interpersonal conflicts	solve problems	interpersonal
depression	feels good about	conflict
helplessness	others	guilt
poor self image	feels satisfied	frustration
hurts self	feels good about	poor self image
loses opportunities	self	hurts others
stress	is good to self	loses
feels out of control	and others	opportunitie
dislikes self and	creates and makes	stress
others	the most of	fells out of
addiction	opportunities	control
loneliness	relaxed	dislikes others
feels angry	feels in control	addiction
	of self	loneliness
	likes self and	feels angry
	others	

* This means long-term effects. The shorter-term effects of
passiveness and aggression are readily seen: passive – turning
off/shutdown; aggressive – outbursts/displays of anger.

Team building

The work of team building is never done. But, how do you go about
it? How do you transform an assembly of individuals into a team?
The team builder (the manager) has very distinctive responsibilities
and these define the role:

- Selection of team members.
- Ensuring that the standards and discipline of the team
  are good so that high performance happens.

- Allocation of responsibilities and control of the use of resources.
- Direction of team strategy and plans.
- Making considerable demands on the team as a group and on individual members.

A pretty onerous set of responsibilities for any manager!

Any team is made up of people working towards a common goal. It is characterised by the way people interact, a sense of collective identity and a group structure. The measure of a team's effectiveness is their capacity to achieve useful results. Effective teams require careful, methodical construction. They can generally perform far beyond that which a collection of individuals can. Specialisation, group dynamics and high performance objectives ensure that the team fulfils its potential. A four-stage cycle has been identified to analyse the working of teams. At each stage the main emphasis changes.

Stage 1 – Forming

The people are not yet a group, but members seek each other out. The group gets used to the task by discussing how to accomplish it, and by making suggestions on the information and resources that will be needed. This is a time for discovering what kind of behaviour is appropriate. Members tend to defer to the leader for guidance.

Stage 2 – Storming

The conflict stage. Members try to express their individuality and resist group pressures and influence. Often emotional responses to the demands being made are felt, especially if the group is under pressure to achieve results.

Stage 3 – Norming

Members develop ways of working together. A sense of group identity begins to emerge. There is a willingness to listen to and accept the views of others. Group standards and members' roles become clear. An effective team is composed of dissimilar people. Members of a team will have their own specialist skills that shape their functional role. They will also have their team role, which relates to their personality. A successful team will have a balance of functional skills and a balance of personalities.

Stage 4 – Performing

The group gets on with its task; solutions are found to problems. The team develops a functional, flexible structure; roles are interrelated. Interpersonal conflicts have been sorted out and the group is highly task orientated. Leadership is a critical part of bringing a group's development to success as an effective team. At the early stages of development, members need feedback, encouragement and reassurance from the leader. The leader will have to clarify objectives, suggest procedures and set standards. Further development requires a positive climate to help the team come through the storming stage. Opportunities need to be created for the team to meet and share information and allow members to take part in the decision-making process.

Checklist for selecting the right team members

Ask yourself these questions when interviewing a prospective new team member. These thoughts could guide you in your questioning. Note there is no '?' column. If in doubt, try to probe a bit more. If you are not satisfied or can't come to a conclusion, then tick the NO column. Three NOs or more, then this person is not for you.

Task	No	Yes
● An alert intelligence?	☐	☐
● A high level of vocational skills?	☐	☐
● Knowledge/skills complement those of other team members rather than duplicate them?	☐	☐
● Motivated to seek excellence in results and methods of working together?	☐	☐
● Honest track record?	☐	☐

Team	No	Yes
● Work closely with others in decision making and problem solving without 'rubbing people up the wrong way'?	☐	☐
● Listen?	☐	☐
● Flexible enough to adopt different roles within the group?	☐	☐
● Influence others – assertive rather than aggressive?	☐	☐
● Contribute to group morale rather than draw upon it?	☐	☐

Individual	No	Yes
● A sense of humour?	☐	☐
● A degree of tolerance for others?	☐	☐
● Will to achieve ambition?	☐	☐
● Understanding that they cannot do it all alone?	☐	☐
● Feeling of responsibility for the success of the team, not simply their own part in it?	☐	☐
● Integrity?	☐	☐
● A realistic perception of own strengths and weaknesses?	☐	☐

Creating the team

Remember we are always working with people and thus need to create the best environment in which the team can grow. There are several factors that need to be considered, especially: who is steering the team?; who is providing the ideas and promoting the team?; and who gets things done? But most important of all is how to get a balanced team. So you need to clearly define:

- the range of tasks
- the resources available
- the skills available.

And also identify:

- strengths (individual and group)
- shortfalls.

The following nine points cover the whole range of how to get the team operating effectively. There may be more than you need but it is worthwhile to have these ideas to hand.

1. **Get a balanced team**
   - Get the right contribution from individuals by using individual abilities, bringing in new abilities, developing latent abilities.
2. **Generate energy**
   - Involve all the team and create enthusiasm.
   - Improve communication.
   - Share responsibility and gain commitment.
   - Create loyalty. Confidence increases with success.
3. **Provide common objectives**
   - Bring together, individual objectives, group objectives and tasks objectives to create a common purpose.
   - Get ideas.

- Create ideas by brainstorming;
- Collect ideas by listening carefully.

4. **Convert ideas to tasks**
   - Constructively criticise ideas and identify creative solutions to problems.

5. **Create an image**
   - Understand what is wanted.
   - Educate those on whom the team rely.

6. **Meet individual needs**
   - Provide opportunities for growth and self-development.
   - Offer a challenge with freedom of action.
   - Encourage greater involvement and personal advancement.

7. **Create an environment**
   - Provide the environment where creativity is encouraged through increased security, flexibility and openness.

8. **Provide coordination**
   - Know what is going on.
   - Know what is wanted.
   - Know/learn how to delegate effectively.

9. **Generate trust**
   Generate trust within and between groups by:
   - recognising individual abilities
   - recognising symbiosis
   - encouraging social contacts
   - generating 'esprit de corps'.

Ultimately, however, it is the manager who looks after the maintenance of the group, who holds it together and provides the push when it is required. When working with people, team building and management is a great challenge and an enormous opportunity for self development for any person.

Conflict management

Leaders often react late and respond ineffectively to conflict. Disputes at work can cause enormous damage to staff morale, performance and customer confidence. But disputes will continue to happen and thrive in an environment of rapid change. An over-dependence on electronic rather than face-to-face communication encourages conflict. Unresolved disputes damage teamwork and performance and create a tense atmosphere. Effective communication becomes difficult.

People feel a bit more secure behind their computer screens and are more prepared to raise issues, challenge inappropriate behaviours and defend their rights, without having a blazing stand-up row. This is a danger that managers must be alert for. The almost silent hidden problems could easily burst out and cause a lot of damage.

Four types of conflict management style have been identified.

1. **Avoider**   For these people conflict is something to be feared, they feel frustrated and hopeless, as they cannot achieve their goals. For avoiders it is easier to withdraw (physically and psychologically) from a conflict than to face it.
2. **Controller**   These people chase their aims regardless. Relationships are unimportant. They think that one side winning and the other losing settles conflicts. They feel that they achieve higher status by winning. Losing makes them feel weak, inadequate and a failure. They try to win by using power; they insist that their way is the only way forward. They simply want to win.
3. **Accommodator**   Some people have a strong need to maintain relationships. When conflict happens they think that their own goals are unimportant. They want conflicts to be resolved quickly to create harmony. They worry that

if the conflict continues, someone will get hurt and that will ruin the relationship.

4. **Collaborator** These people view a conflict as a problem to be solved. They are good at seeing other people's point of view, without forgetting their own goals. They are not satisfied until solutions have been found and the tensions and negative feelings have been resolved.

So, what is your conflict resolution style? When working with people it pays to have some idea of how the group or the people involved operate because conflict cultures are often set by the most influential people. Most managers will adopt a range of styles. Of those outlined a more collaborative approach to conflict management and dispute resolution is probably best. When difficult issues occur, make sure that you:

- stay impartial
- listen to all sides before identifying key concerns and issues
- ask people to say what they need, rather than what they want
- consider the benefit of settling amicably against risk of continuing the dispute
- tailor your approach to achieve the best results.

Here are some suggestions for core values for effective dispute resolution:

- fairness
- consistency of how you do it
- minimum skill standards
- equal time to both sides
- resolve disputes as close as possible to the source of the conflict
- seek mutually acceptable outcomes where possible

- help people identify key issues, and resolve disputes in teams
- provide a robust process when issues need to be dealt with formally.

Be alert when working with people, as disputes can very often be predicted. Don't wait for them to happen and be caught napping. Any silly little thing can spark off conflict and disputes. If you take a proactive approach you are much more likely to get better ideas for solutions to conflict. But above all, keep trust under pressure – and survive! You will find more on dealing with formal disputes in Chapter 10.

Negotiation skills

Few people have good negotiating skills. Reluctance to negotiate, make counter-proposals and concessions are made worse by lack of practice. We don't like confrontation and are concerned that we may be made to look foolish. This inability to negotiate is damaging. We need intense training and practice.

Starting

Don't be afraid to negotiate, but don't negotiate if you don't have to. Negotiating skills will give you power if you have none to start with.

You lose nothing by asking for a better deal – most things are negotiable. First proposals are rarely the best but, to improve upon them, you do have to ask. Don't just complain; propose solutions or remedies.

There are only three rules for a successful negotiation: prepare, prepare, and prepare! So prepare fully, and with care. Don't negotiate if you are not prepared, time is needed to plan, check assumptions and test them. Preparation and planning are the keys to successful negotiation.

Negotiation basics

There are six basic steps in negotiating:

1. Getting to know one another

Take a little time to get to know one another, and assess those involved. You can judge the level of importance placed on the issues, and the degree of expertise engaged. Start by observing, listening and learning. Keep the beginning friendly and relaxed, yet businesslike.

2. Stating goals and objectives

After opening, start with a general statement of goals and objectives by the parties involved, but don't state specific issues. Each party is beginning to explore the needs of the other. No terms are being suggested yet, but positive statements made on behalf of an agreement being reached are favourable to all concerned. If there are differences, now is the time to know about them. Make the initial statements positive and agreeable; this is not time for hostility or defensiveness. Try to build an atmosphere of co-operation and mutual trust. Try to estimate the level of authority that your negotiating partner has. Knowing this could avoid frustrating delays in the closing stages.

3. Starting the process

Negotiations are often complex with many issues to resolve; others have only a few. Of course, individual issues vary greatly in complexity. You cannot predict the direction a negotiation will take until both parties have presented the issues. There may be hidden needs neither party has raised; these will surface as things proceed.

Often issues are joined together, the solution to one being dependent on the solution to another. There may be an attempt to separate issues. A skilled negotiator will study the issues closely before negotiations begin, to determine where advantages lie – whether to split or combine issues.

The negotiators will review the issues then deal with them one by one. Some feel negotiation should start with a minor issue that has the potential of being easily resolved. This will establish a favourable climate for additional agreements. Others feel that beginning with a major issue is best; unless it is satisfactorily resolved, the others are not important.

4. Expressions of disagreement and conflict

Once the issues have been defined, disagreement and conflict will often occur. This is natural and should be expected. Never try to avoid this phase; the process of give and take is where successful deals are made

Disagreement, if handled properly, will eventually bring negotiators together. If handled poorly, they will widen the differences. Conflict brings out different points of view, and identifies the real wants and needs of the negotiators.

When presenting the issues, most negotiators will explain what they want. The other negotiator must find out what they need, or will settle for. Few negotiators will get all they want, even in a successful negotiation. Good negotiators work to get as much as possible, understanding that compromise is necessary, and you may need to change your goals.

Confrontation can involve stress. Conflict resolution is not a test of power but an opportunity to find out what people need. Properly handled, this should lead to areas of agreement or compromise.

5. Reassessment and compromise

At some point, one party will move towards compromise. Statements reflecting this often begin with words like 'Suppose that...?', 'What if...?', 'How would you feel about...?'. When these statements begin, listen carefully; is an attempt to compromise being offered? State the response carefully. Too quick an attempt to pin something down may cause the other party to withdraw; the time may not seem right to giving and getting.

When responding to offers, it is a good practice to restate them. This has at least three advantages:

● The offer may be improved; the other party may get the impression that your echo is a negative.

● The offerer may attempt justification. This will provide opportunities for challenge.

● An echo gives you time to think about a counter offer. However, if the other negotiator echoes your offer, simply confirm it, don't sweeten it. Confirmation forces the other negotiator to accept it, reject it, or suggest an alternative.

6. Agreement in principle or settlement

When agreement is reached, confirm it. A decision about how the final settlement will be obtained is essential, especially if higher approval is required. Put the agreed terms in writing while the parties are together, so they can agree on the language. There is then less danger of misunderstandings later.

Agreement is the ultimate objective of any negotiation. Identify the level of authority of the party you are negotiating with, at the outset. People will negotiate in order to identify your position, then tell you they do not have the authority to accept your terms. Then they go to some other person who could well reject the tentative 'agreement' in an attempt to manoeuvre a better deal. When you have the authority to make an agreement, try to negotiate with a person who has the same level of authority.

Types of negotiators

Some negotiators set out to deliberately unsettle you; whatever they do, the main objective is to persuade you to concede more. They may be aggressive, friendly, warm or cold. You will recognise some of these people from situations other than negotiations. People do not conform to a common mould, you will know this from generally working with people, So be aware of what they are doing, and why.

The aggressive opener

This is a negotiating style that starts almost before the negotiators have sat down. The idea is to discomfort and wrong foot the opposition from the word go, by making them feel extremely uncomfortable.

The long pause negotiator

This style of negotiation relies on one negotiator listening to the other, not immediately answering propositions that they put, and appearing to give them considerable thought, with the result that there are long silences. It is most effective in the early to middle stages of the negotiation. The style works best when there is a little tension in the air; people are feeling on edge and find the length of the silence embarrassing, thus creating more tension.

The purpose is to get the other side to reveal as much of their case and argument as possible, while giving away as little of one's own as possible. Some negotiators prolong the silence by appearing to take extensive notes of what has been said; they deliberately delay the need to make any reply until they have everything fully written down.

Deriding

Deriding the opposition's proposals is another way of causing discomfort. The objective is to get the other side so irritated that they say something that they will later regret. It is best employed when the opposition are putting forward their proposals; the response, verbal and non-verbal, suggests that they do not really know what they are talking about.

The interrogator

Negotiation by interrogation has the objective of finding out the opposition's position. Proposals get searching questions, put in a way that makes the opposition feel that they have not done their homework thoroughly. Its success depends on a style of questioning that aims to confuse rather than enlighten. Any unclear answers are immediately challenged and the opposition asked to explain more clearly what they mean.

Reasonableness

Reasonableness is a disguise for the negotiator who appears to be agreeable and helpful, but makes impossible demands. The style has a quiet, well-modulated voice with an agreeable and pleasant manner. The whole purpose of this style is to win the friendship and confidence of the opposition. This is done by being pleasant and courteous; demonstrating understanding of their position, but they really must see the problem from his point of view, just as he does from theirs.

Divide and conquer

The purpose of divide and conquer is to produce conflict among the opposition. The negotiating team pays more attention to its own internal disagreements than to disagreements with the opposition. They try tactics to ally themselves with one member of the team to play off against colleagues. This person imagines having some success and skill as a negotiator, building up the relationship with the opposition, enhancing self-esteem and the feel-good factor. Colleagues see unwillingness to move. The whole process builds up considerable internal tensions within the negotiation team which can be resolved by the apparently intransigent members agreeing with the other side. To create such an alliance, the negotiator employs all sorts of techniques that have as their objective the flattering of the other person.

Stupid

This negotiator pretends to be particularly dense and exasperates the opposition by pretending not to understand what the other side is saying and asking questions to which the answers seem obvious, or have already been given. The style needs to be kept up for some time so that the levels of irritation build up. This negotiator hopes that someone in the opposing team will crack trying to find increasingly simple ways to describe proposals; each proposal being elaborated and amplified so that it can be fully understood.

In dealing with these negotiating styles, the problem will mostly be resolved when you realise what is going on. Let the nonsense wash over you and enjoy the performance! Or perhaps expose the other side by commenting that these tactics do not work with you.

Negotiation preparation

There will be many questions that you need to answer. Note your answers as you go through the preparation stage, before the actual negotiation meeting. Your initial answers may change in response to extra information, or in response to changes in your needs. Make changes, probe in detail; in that way your preparation will be as comprehensive as possible.

Define goals and objectives

- Exactly what do I want from this negotiation?
- What do I have to get to meet my needs?
- What am I willing to give up to get what I want?

- What are my time and economic constraints for this negotiation?

Clarify the issues

- What are the issues as I see them now?
- What is the background to my position?
- How will I present it to the other party?
- What are the issues as I want them to be seen by the other party?
- How will they present their own position?
- What seem to be the significant differences in the way the parties view the issues?

Gather information

- Who will I be negotiating with and what do I know about them?
- How do they approach a negotiation?
- What are their ego needs?
- When and where will the negotiation take place?
- What advantages or disadvantages do the alternatives have for me? For the other party?
- What are the economic, political and human implications of the issues?
- What personal power do I have that can be used constructively in this negotiation?

Humanise and set the climate

- How can I best establish rapport with the other party?
- How can I establish a win/win climate?

Prepare for conflict

- What will be the major points of conflict?
- How will I determine what the other party needs as compared with what they want?

Compromise/resolution of the issues

- How will I attempt to resolve conflict?
- How will I respond to the other party's attempts to resolve conflict?
- What concessions am I prepared to make?
- Do I know what my concession limits are?
- Under what conditions?
- What do I expect in return for my concessions?

Agreement and confirmation

- How formal must it be?
- What approval process will be required?
- How long will it take?
- What implementation steps will be needed?

It is best to use the checklist below with your team, when you are together preparing for the coming negotiation meeting. Not all the points will be relevant for you for any one negotiation, but the whole set provides a useful framework on which to build and consolidate a logical discussion. You will be better prepared for the sequence of events that will follow if you have thoroughly explored all these points and tried out your negotiating skills on each other.

For many people negotiating is not easy – or pleasant. But it is a fact of everyday working life and, without realising it, we are continually in negotiating situations – even as trivial as 'What shall we do for lunch? ... No, I want to do some shopping.' In a workaday context, practice makes (if not perfect, then ...) better. The more practice you get, the better your negotiating skills become. Practice plus preparation will make for increasing success in your negotiations.

Negotiation check list

Negotiation can be a lengthy process. Start with information gathering, then team preparation, then practice. This checklist will help both before and during negotiation sessions.

- Remember the opening five minutes is the critical time.
- Maintain your awareness – the other side is watching you.
- Do not make assumptions at any point; always confirm statements.
- Your preparation will have identified ways of satisfying the needs of the other side, as well as your own.
- Keep up the pressure of your own demands.
- Avoid provocation – irritators, your own defensive spiral, or their immediate counter-offers, all weaken your position.
- Build coalitions, make 'friends' with one or more of the other side.
- Probe discreetly, listen effectively, then play back your understanding, summarise.
- Security of your own information is priority.
- Advance single reasons for proof with incremental disclosure.
- Express your feelings – messages are very useful.
- Lateral thinking will help to put the arguments of both sides in perspective.
- Finally, patience will get you the result you want.

These negotiating ideas will help to keep your thoughts on the matter in focus. It is all too easy to go off track in the course of a complex negotiation. This checklist will be a useful aide memoire.

Leadership

Leadership is the projection of personality. It is a combination of persuasion and compulsion. The basic ingredients are courage, will power, knowledge, judgement, adaptability, initiative and integrity. Good leadership gets people to want to do what we want them to do.

Characteristics of a good leader

- **Inner drive** Has a powerful urge to get things done, to organise, to take responsibility.
- **Intelligence** More intelligent, but is not 'superior' about it. Must be a good communicator.
- **Maturity and openness of mind** Emotionally balanced, aware of most innate prejudices and hostilities. Never afraid that new ideas might threaten. Judgement is balanced, can make confident decisions.
- **Attitude to people** Knows that the job is done through people. Approaches problems in terms of the people involved rather than technical difficulties. Tries to preserve and develop human dignity. The 'servant' of subordinates, and assumes personal responsibility for what they do and how they work. Not afraid to be 'tough' with people when occasion demands it, but toughness for emergencies rather than to disguise lack of confidence.

Here are some 'golden rules' for good leadership:

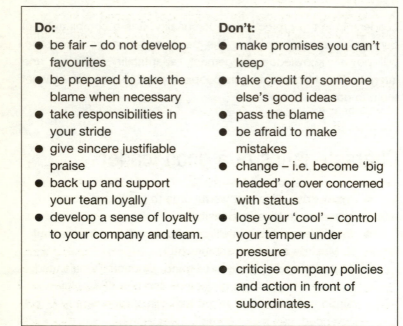

Do:
- be fair – do not develop favourites
- be prepared to take the blame when necessary
- take responsibilities in your stride
- give sincere justifiable praise
- back up and support your team loyally
- develop a sense of loyalty to your company and team.

Don't:
- make promises you can't keep
- take credit for someone else's good ideas
- pass the blame
- be afraid to make mistakes
- change – i.e. become 'big headed' or over concerned with status
- lose your 'cool' – control your temper under pressure
- criticise company policies and action in front of subordinates.

Types of authority

A leader must develop as much authority as possible, maintain that authority and use it effectively. Do not make the mistake of thinking that authority is something that arises solely from your title, your position in the organisation or your job description. There are different types of authority, all of which are relevant in industry or commerce.

Structural authority

Based on the position a person holds within the structure of an organisation, e.g. job description and responsibility in industry.

The important thing for a leader to know is how to use the structural authority that you have. The golden rules are 'don't use it all unless you have to', be careful 'not to exceed the structural authority that you have', and 'ensure that the subordinates are in no doubt as to its extent and implications'.

Knowledge authority

Based on the knowledge, skill and experience of the individual. To maintain this authority a leader should:

- keep in touch with his or her subordinates and their work
- keep up to date with technical developments and new ideas
- go on relevant training courses.

There is really nothing wrong with a team member having more technical skill or knowledge than their manager. If this is the case do not pretend to have knowledge authority that you do not really have. If you decide that you need to increase such authority then ask questions of your people and your own managers. Also have some formal training.

Moral authority

Based on the integrity and 'goodness' of the individual. It is behaviour rather than knowledge or position that gives rise to moral authority. It is acquired from the respect your people have for you. To increase this:

- keep your word
- give credit when due
- show respect for people and treat them well
- be considerate
- treat your staff fairly but firmly and equally
- practise what you preach

- combine self confidence with modesty
- be genuine, natural and relaxed.

Charismatic authority

Based on the personality and natural powers of leadership of the individual. Charisma is to a large extent 'born not made'. Some people are natural leaders and some are not, however we should all make the most of what we have. This means appearing to your people as confident in yourself and your decisions; an effective communicator, well turned out, cool under pressure, well organised, enthusiastic and a source of strength and encouragement in times of trouble.

These four types of authority are the means by which you can exert influence. A good leader will rarely, if ever, use structural authority to get things done. Poor leaders, on the other hand, will depend on it. This will make them a worse leader still.

Other types of authority

- **Physical authority** Based on the obvious or implied physical superiority of the individual, e.g. the 'hard man'.
- **Statutory authority** Based on the backing of legal powers, e.g. inspectors of all sorts, judges, police etc.
- **Parental authority** Based on the special relationship which exists between parent and child.
- **Clerical authority** Based on the relationship which exists between religious appointees and laypeople.
- **Economic authority** Based on the control of money or material possessions.

Leader versus Driver

Some people are leaders, with an innate sense of how to carry out their job. Some are drivers who may have personality problems that show in their attitudes and how they do their job. Here are some comparisons:

The Leader:	The Driver:
● Motivates by increasing satisfaction	● Motivates by fear through threats of decreasing satisfaction.
● Trusts his/her employees.	● Trusts no one.
● Delegates authority whenever possible.	● Always demonstrates his/her own authority.
● Gives reasons for orders and instructions.	● Expects orders to be obeyed blindly and without question.
● Gives credit where due.	● Takes credit to him/herself.
● Exercises power through people.	● Exercises power over people.
● Believes that most people want to do a good job if given the opportunity.	● Believes that no one will do a good job unless forced to do so.
● Sees the workforce as human beings, who can be trusted to put their hearts into the task.	● Sees employees as replaceable production units who can only be persuaded by fear or by appeals to the lowest form of self-interest.
● Maintains discipline which people respect.	● Maintains a discipline that is defensive and which people fear.
● Inspires loyalty and initiative	● Demands blind obedience.

We must learn to recognise these traits in others – and in ourselves! There are significant differences between the true leader and the taskmaster (driver). In the short term the driver may seem to be more successful, but will lose out to the real leader over the long run.

Here is a well-known and significant statement about leadership:

A leader is best
When people scarcely know that he exists.
Not so good when they blindly obey and acclaim him,
Worse when they despise him.
Fail to honour people
They fail to honour you.
But of a good leader, who talks little,
When his work is done, his aim fulfilled,
They will all say, 'We did this ourselves'.

Lao Tse (c. 500BC)

Elements of leadership

The table opposite contains a list of elements of the leader's role in brief. To decide how good/bad you are at each of them, rank (1, 2, 3) your three strongest areas in the left-hand column and your three weakest areas in the right-hand column. For the purposes of this questionnaire, ignore factors outside your control, and concentrate on your own personal style of working with people.

Strongest	Leadership element	Weakest
	Hiring the right people for the right jobs.	
	Organising the work of your team so that they work well together.	
	Directing your staff by initial induction and training and target setting.	
	Motivating them to give of their best.	
	Controlling your team by giving them the right kind of supervision.	
	Correcting your staff when they go astray in either technical or disciplinary matters.	
	Assisting those on your team who need either personal or technical help.	
	Developing your staff to make the most of their abilities and potential abilities.	
	Decision making so as to get the best possible decision in the available time.	
	Changing systems and procedures when necessary and overcoming resistance to change.	
	Inspiring your team when things are going badly.	
	Retaining those staff who are good performers.	
	Firing those staff who are bad performers.	

Commentary

This is an interesting test of self-integrity. The idea of thinking about your strongest and weakest leadership characteristics is simply that – to get you thinking. We generally accept the things we do in our job, without any real analysis; it's something we do. But in relation to working with people and our leadership style, it is worth considering how well we do some things, how poorly we may do others.

To take just a few examples: some of us pull back from any degree of personal conflict, so we may not be very good at 'correcting', or 'controlling', or 'firing'. Some of us may be very good at 'organising', or 'directing', or even 'motivating', but have we got the right training and background knowledge to be good at 'hiring'?

Obviously the leadership elements mentioned need a great deal of amplification and we cover many of them in this book. But for now, just spend a little while pondering 'how am I doing?'. Maybe if you can identify strengths you will be able to build on them – 'I am really good at "assisting"'; think about this; are you really assisting, or just doing it for them? Similarly, examine the whole list and be as self-critical as you can. Nobody else will know about it, unless you want them to. And the process might just make you a bit better as a leader.

SUMMARY

One of the main functions that any manager has to deal with is problem solving. This and other matters are dealt with in this chapter.

The ability to solve problems effectively is a real plus point in any manager's competence index. It requires good knowledge of the subject and a quick grasp of what the people involved need. To avoid conflict, the manager needs to be able to adopt an assertive style of leadership, to reassure the team that all is under control and that the situation will be cleared up, the problem solved to the satisfaction of all.

That is an idealistic scenario; in practice, problem solving can be difficult and a manager may need to use all the techniques discussed in this chapter to reach a harmonious conclusion. The manager, to succeed in working with people, will have developed both an effective team and a leadership style that will ensure cooperation in problem solving without the potential damaging effects of workplace conflict.

09

What about meetings?

Meetings are an essential part of everyday working life. But many meetings are unnecessary, unproductive and often waste time. Think carefully before setting up a meeting and don't call a meeting to decide something you could and should decide yourself. And never get people together if some other method would serve your purpose. Remember, their time is your money; effective meetings are essential for good management.

Good meetings are planned, they don't just happen. They start well before the participants assemble, and continue after they leave.

Run properly meetings can be an effective means of:

- communicating to a group
- meeting people face to face
- improving the quality of decisions
- getting to know people
- drawing from a variety of different experiences
- building teams.

Before the meeting

Consider who you are going to invite. What will they have to contribute by way of information, opinion or assistance in the decision making? If they are not needed, don't invite them. If you are invited to a meeting, apply the same criteria to your own attendance: if it comes out negatively, decline or send a well-briefed subordinate. This will save your time, and will give your subordinate good experience in attending meetings.

Think out the agenda carefully. Define the purpose of the meeting and state it clearly: e.g., to analyse, inform, decide, coordinate. Put the purpose at the top of your invitation memo. Likewise, if you receive an invitation to a meeting that does not state a purpose, query it. If you don't get a satisfactory answer don't go; don't waste your time.

Now organise the agenda. Prioritise the items, and give a very brief (no more than 10–12 words) statement why each item is included. Put a time limit on each item for discussion according to its importance. There should be no surprises, so those attending will have the opportunity to be prepared for the topic and contribute usefully. Send the agenda out in good time; not too early since people forget, but not too late – don't provide an excuse for coming to the meeting unprepared. If the invitation that you receive is not clear as to topics and timing, seek clarification and ask approximately when the items in which you are involved will come up.

This leads to the idea of staggering the attendance; there is usually no need for everybody to be there all the time. Note beside each agenda item who will be involved. Try to group items together that concern an individual; get them dealt with, then they can go. It will not always work but, if they know the timing, people can come in when their item is due for discussion, slip out when it is finished, and return if need be later on. It is amazing what can be done in 15 or 30 minutes when you are not being bored in an ineffective meeting.

The timing of any meeting is important. It will be impossible to find a time that will suit everyone but, if adequate notice is given, participants will be able to organise themselves to attend without having to disrupt their schedules. Try not to hold 'emergency' meetings; but if an emergency does arise hold a 'stand-up' meeting – don't sit down – brief people quickly on the problem and then send out 'action minutes'. These will indicate: the problem; the action to be taken (the solution?), who is responsible, and date/time for feedback. This is also called an 'Action Meeting' (see below).

Try to hold your meetings somewhere other than in your office; if this is not possible, make sure you avoid interruptions. Put a Do Not Disturb sign on the door, disconnect the phone and make yourself unavailable. Let your secretary or colleagues know when you will be free. With such excellent pre-planning you will be able to tell exactly when this will be.

During the meeting

Start on time. Don't penalise those arriving on time and reward latecomers by waiting for them. A good chairman will be in control of the meeting at all times, and starting on time is a vital control point.

Organise the minute taking and the time keeping. It is best not to take minutes yourself, since you need to concentrate on direction and not interrupt the flow. An independent reminder of the times you pre-set for discussion is also valuable and is a good discipline for yourself. This is particularly important if people are to join the meeting at various times. Good orchestration of a meeting generally means that it will be effective and that things will get done.

Start with and stick to the agenda; don't be side-tracked. How you handle discussion of the topics will depend on the purpose of the meeting – to inform, generate creative solutions, or decide;

different styles of chairmanship will be appropriate. But always remember the time limits that you set and the purpose of the meeting; remind everyone of this frequently.

At the end of each item – and also at the end of the meeting – summarise, get agreement as to whether the purpose has been achieved, state conclusions, and action assignments if relevant.

Be fair to all participants. Encourage the shy, firmly stop the garrulous. Politely give all the opportunity to speak, but do not allow the meeting to get off track and away from the agenda. Remember the purpose and do all you can to achieve the objectives.

End on time; respect the plans of those who have assumed that it will and have trusted you to achieve this aim.

After the meeting

Evaluate it for your own benefit, being as objective as you possibly can. Ask:

- Was the advance information adequate?
- Did the meeting start on time?
- Was the agenda followed, and was the purpose achieved in the time allocated?
- Were the right people in attendance?
- Was time wasted?

There could be more questions, but this self-evaluation is a useful learning tool for improving meeting effectiveness.

Then make sure the minutes are sent out within two days of the meeting; the quicker the better. Minutes should be concise; they are not a verbatim record of the discussion: only decisions, those responsible for taking action, and deadlines are needed. The rest is just padding. Follow up on decisions and check what progress has been made – are there any reports, and what action has been taken to implement decisions?

Finally ask: Is your meeting really necessary? Make a list of meetings, apply the criteria of achievement of purpose and implementation of decisions. If the meetings pass the acid test, they can continue. If they fail disband the committee concerned, and don't allow new ones to reform by inertia. Get rid of what is unnecessary; you will save a lot of time and ensure much more effective meetings.

Reminders for successful meetings

- Hold them only if they are really needed or necessary (Ask yourself if people could be told any other way?)
- Set a purpose
    - What do you want to achieve?
    - What decisions need to be made?
    - What actions need to be taken?
- Consider the costs
    - Meetings aren't cheap (time away from job, salaries of those attending etc.)
- Prepare an agenda
    - Include only relevant items.
    - Put them in order of importance.
    - Allocate time for each.
- Collect all information
    - If it's lengthy summarise it, outlining key points.
    - Send out agendas and key points in advance.
    - Only invite those affected by topics under discussion.

Checklist for running the meeting

Use this checklist as an aide-memoire during the meeting and as the basis for review following the meeting.

Have I done this?	No	Yes
● Have I told everyone the purpose of the meeting?	☐	☐
● Have I set the scene before each item, e.g. by opening discussion and inviting specific contributions from those present?	☐	☐
● Has everyone who has something to say made a contribution?	☐	☐
● Have I summarised (but not let them go on so long as to dominate the discussion) what has been said as the meeting proceeds?	☐	☐
● Have I ensured that there is a record or notes taken?	☐	☐
● Have I watched for signs for non-participation and encouraged the quiet people to come in?	☐	☐
● Have I kept to time? (Always start on time and don't be afraid to finish early.)	☐	☐
● Have I agreed actions to follow and allocated responsibility for taking action?	☐	☐
● Don't be afraid to critique the meeting, either by yourself or with your team:		
– Was it worth it?	☐	☐
– What could I have done differently?	☐	☐
● After the meeting		
– Have I circulated the minutes to those attending and interested parties? (Preferably in less than one week.)	☐	☐
– Have I monitored and reviewed progress of any actions decided?	☐	☐

Action meetings

Action meetings are appropriate at all levels of management. They are useful time savers and can replace general meetings (or information gatherings) already being held either to discuss the same subjects, or to make quick decisions in an emergency situation.

Action meetings are convened at operational level by supervisors, for the people reporting to them. The people involved will be thus directly concerned with the incident.

The purpose of an action meeting is to:

- identify a problem (perhaps already evident)
- decide on action to be taken
- by whom
- by when.

Action meetings should be informal, important and practical. They will often be set up in a hurry to deal with an incident that needs urgent attention. There will thus generally be a lot of pressure. Here are some requirements for success.

Procedure

- The meeting should be held by the person who is responsible for the department and receives the control or incident report and who, as chairperson should know the facts behind the problem. For the meeting to be a success good briefing is essential.
- The meetings should be strictly confined to getting the facts and making decisions. Involved discussions of detail should be done elsewhere. Any counselling of

individuals that may be necessary should also be done elsewhere.

- The agenda should also form the minutes, and should be in the form of an Action Statement. This means a minimum of work and that all the information is on the same piece of paper.

- The first subjects to be considered at any meeting should be those overdue from previous meetings. By this automatic follow-up, outstanding items get priority attention.

- Meetings should be short, decisive and to the point. They may even be held standing up.

Effectiveness and success criteria

- The effectiveness of Action Meetings depends very much on the chairperson competence. The chairperson has to learn how to conduct them. Their success determines the usefulness of the management control system.

- The chairperson should:
  - Be positive – encourage suggestions for improvement (and listen to them!).
  - Not allow post mortems. (We can learn valuable lessons from the past, and do better in the future. But don't overdo it.) Action meetings are not for allotting blame.
  - Be obviously interested in the situation, not use pressure and never give offence.
  - Never ridicule members. Disciplining should be done away from the meeting. (Be careful, questioning the chairperson may get a team member to admit mistakes to their colleagues.)

(You will recognise the attitudes advocated here in your task of working with people.)

Other areas of charing Action Meetings are similar to chairing any meeting and include:

- The ability to keep the meeting to the point.
- The ability to persuade the meeting to the chairperson's viewpoint; but the chairperson must be flexible in accepting other points of view.
- The ability to get sound decisions made.
- The ability to get people to commit themselves to take action.
- The ability to instil a sense of purpose, or even urgency, into discussions.

The main advantage of action meetings is their immediacy. If a problem arises, a quick creative solution can be found and monitored. Action meetings should be ad hoc, as and when needed. They are one of the most effective ways of solving problems and not wasting time.

Here are some thoughts to consider

- Do I hold regular action meetings? (Only when really needed.)
- If no, should I hold them to ensure action? (Too often and you lose the sense of urgency.)
- Do they get action or are they talking shops? (My job is to stick to the point and get action.)
- Is anyone there who shouldn't be? (If so, ask them to leave.)
- Is anyone absent who should be there? (If they are not, find them!)
- Are we positive at all times? (Stick to the point; only discuss the urgent matter.)
- Do we reach positive decisions about what to do, by when, by whom? (This is what we are gathered to do.)

- Do we issue an Action Statement to Control Action? (Always!)
- Do we avoid recriminations, history? (Absolutely. We discuss the immediate problem only.)
- Do we keep to the point? (Again, absolutely, otherwise we waste time, money and energy – and the problem could get worse as we talk.)

Checklist for running an action meeting

- Tell everyone the purpose. ☐
- Set the scene for each item, e.g. open discussion by inviting specific contributions from those present. ☐
- Let everyone who has something to say make a contribution (but watch windbags!). ☐
- Watch for signs of non-participation. (Encourage, by open questions.) ☐
- Summarise what has been said as the meeting proceeds. Record and ensure minutes are taken accurately. ☐
- Stick to time. (Always start on time and don't be afraid to finish early.) ☐
- Agree actions to follow. ☐
- Don't be afraid to critique the meeting
  - Was it worth it? ☐
  - What could you have done differently? ☐
- After the meeting
  - Circulate minutes to those attending and interested parties. ☐
  - Monitor and review progress of any actions decided. ☐

Action Statement

Date: _____

Department: _____

Present: _____(Chairperson)

No:	Item for action	Date raised	Action agreed	By whom	By when	Follow-up

SUMMARY

This chapter has examined one of the main bugbears of a managers' life – meetings! But regrettably, there they are, so it is best to know how to run them efficiently, to ensure that the time, money and effort expended gets effective results.

There are right ways (and wrong ways!) to manage meetings. They involve planning, good communications before, during and after the event; scrupulous chairmanship, attention to detail and above all regard and respect for the people involved. Running an effective meeting is not easy; this chapter has given some ideas as to how to make it work well.

What are the best ways to solve disputes?

Any organisation is a human structure; it is built around individuals but must be strong enough to survive one or more people leaving it. The aim of good people management must be to create a set of skilled teams where the value of the team is of greater worth than that of the individuals in the team. However, sooner or later some people will leave. The process of leaving must be dealt with carefully or it may lead to difficulties for both the organisation and the individual. Most people will leave voluntarily, for clear and unavoidable reasons. In some cases though, the reasons may not be very clear. It is important to have a leaving interview as soon as possible after their resignation notice to find out the real reason for leaving. Apart from redundancy, for which there are specific rules, some people will leave involuntarily because of their performance, or for other reasons. The key to these cases is to identify the problem as early as possible, to try to enable that person to overcome their difficulties. It is no kindness to someone with a particular problem to overlook it. If you don't do anything about the problem you may soon get to the point of termination; it is then too late to put matters right. Cases of misconduct are difficult; the organisation should have a clear policy on discipline and grievance issues, which has to be applied.

It is your job in working with people to be aware of, and become confident with, the rules and regulations that your company has established. Although there are core premises for dealing with disputes, discipline and grievances, each organisation will have its own variations; you will need to thoroughly understand the particular set of rules that your company has adopted. In Chapter 7 we looked at how to deal with conflict in the early stages; here we look at more formal grievance or dispute situations.

Establishing rules

Every organisation should have a mode of procedure, which governs day-to-day operations. It should be:

- clearly stated in everyday language, avoiding legalese, so it can be easily understood
- fair and reasonable, in line with best practice
- able to be revised if necessary, to deal with changing circumstances
- explained to those it applies to and what the consequences of breaking the rules will be.

Where rule breaking occurs, appropriate disciplinary or corrective procedures need to be applied. Disciplinary procedures could be provided for action in cases of dishonesty, breaking safety rules, persistent lateness, insubordination, absenteeism or any other abuses of a tolerant system.

You really need to familiarise yourself with the disciplinary and grievance procedures that your company has in place. Naturally you will hope never to have to resort to using them, but in working with people there is never the certainly of smooth running and it is always good to be prepared.

Disciplinary procedures

There are a number of essential features of disciplinary procedures.

- They must be in writing and specify to whom they apply. This is important because there could be different levels of action for different levels of employee.
- They must specify who will take the disciplinary action. This will define your role.
- They give an indication of what disciplinary action will ensue and what will be involved.
- They will provide for people to be:
  - informed of complaints
  - investigated
  - represented when the matter is heard by any tribunal.
- They provide a system of recording procedures for reference.
- They provide a procedure for erasing records should the case be dismissed.

In any dispute at work it is very sensible to seek the participation of the Human Resources (HR) department. Your own authority will only extend to your immediate work area and responsibilities. Disciplinary or grievance action may well go outside these limits; therefore advice from HR is necessary.

Establishing your own authority

This means having an acceptable, legal power structure. You need clear terms of reference and powers which are acknowledged. It is your job to ensure that staff are knowledgeable, well informed and trained in the procedures they have to carry out. You will look to develop staff that have the appropriate personal qualities. These will include the ability to be:

- diplomatic, especially in situations where there may be some tension
- well organised and exemplary in their conduct
- fair and show concern for their fellow workers.

You will have trained them to be good listeners, who will be able to accept the thinking behind the rules and procedures with which they have to work.

Discipline and grievance procedures

It is important to understand the difference in these two structures. They both need to be handled with empathy; disciplinary situations will concern you more directly, grievance situations may arise out of matters over which you have no control.

Disciplinary issues arise where you, as manager, have concerns about an employee's conduct, absence from work or the way in which they are doing their job. You may start a disciplinary procedure that could lead to disciplinary action, potentially including dismissal in more serious cases. This is not an easy course to take and you should exhaust all other means of influencing the offending employee before taking the disciplinary action step. Your company will have a system of warnings of increasing severity. These will give you the opportunity to negotiate the problem. However, this may not succeed, so you must be prepared and know about how disciplinary proceedings are carried out.

Grievances, on the other hand, concern problems or complaints that an employee raises with the employer. They cover, for example, concerns about the job, terms and conditions, contractual or statutory rights, or the way they feel they are being treated at work. If the problem is a grievance, you will probably be approached in the first place. Listen carefully to the complaint but if, as is likely, you are unable to solve the problem as it is not within your control, then bring in the HR department quickly. They are the expert conciliators and it is best that you do not get embroiled in a grievance dispute.

How to handle disciplinary issues

You may become aware of a problem with one of your people. Talk to them about your concern. Keep this conversation informal at first because the problem may be the result of a misunderstanding, and you could get evidence to clarify the issue. You should, however, keep a note of the conversation and what was agreed. If talking does not work, you may decide to go directly to formal disciplinary and dismissal procedures. The next step should be to write to the person setting out the complaint made against them. This should include sufficient information about the alleged misconduct or poor performance so that they have the opportunity to prepare a response or an explanation before a formal meeting.

You now need to arrange the meeting at a reasonable time and place to discuss the issue. You should not take any disciplinary action before this meeting. Remember that your worker has a statutory right to ask someone to accompany them to the meeting – either a colleague from work or a trade union representative. You should give your employee the opportunity to set out their side of the argument at the meeting. After the meeting has concluded you must tell them what has been decided; you should do this in writing.

This can become a long and tiresome process, but it is the law and you have to abide by it. It is wise therefore to think very hard before starting on any formal disciplinary procedure because, even after all the talking, meeting and deciding the employee has the right to appeal; the whole thing can escalate into an unpleasant mess. Depending on the nature of the incident there is likely to be some publicity that could possibly be damaging to yourself and your company. In deciding to go ahead you should be prepared to face this possibility.

If the employee does not agree with your decision, they need to write to you and tell you that they are appealing your decision. They need to explain why they do not agree with it. You will now have to arrange a further meeting to discuss the appeal. Again, they have a statutory right to have someone to accompany them to the meeting. Make sure you take notes at the appeal meeting; write to your employee to let them know your final decision.

You may reverse or amend your original decision in the light of any new evidence presented or, of course, you may maintain your original decision. This will probably not please the employee so you may want to offer them some other options to consider as a means of finally resolving the dispute. This is going to take you outside the abilities of your own HR department and colleagues. It will also bring you into public view – and it is going to cost money.

Dealing with grievances

The actual procedure for handling grievances is very much the same as for disciplinary proceedings. But the emphasis is different; the complaint is coming about you from the employee. Neither process is comfortable, but in this case you are being compelled to defend yourself from what may be serious allegations. So again we are into the routine of: talk; write; meet; appeal – and this time it may be you who is in the dock!

Generally the first thing you will know about anyone raising a grievance is in an informal meeting (which may be acrimonious) with the person to whom you are the immediate manager. They obviously will want to explain their concerns. If you can, you may find it helpful to suggest what you would like them to do to resolve their problem. It may be difficult or embarrassing to talk to your own immediate manager, but you could speak to someone else in the organisation who is in a position of authority.

If you cannot resolve the grievance by talking directly to the employee, the next thing to do is to consider using your company's formal procedures for grievances. You should be able to find these in your Company Handbook or Personnel manual.

In all grievance cases it is essential that everything be written down. Accurate notes (not just minutes) of what is said at a meeting are vital – they may be used as evidence at a later date. So write to the complainant with your understanding of the grievance. Your letter should be dated; keep a copy of this and all other correspondence. If you have not done so already, it may be helpful to suggest to them how you would like to resolve the problem. An initial meeting should be arranged at a reasonable time and place with all parties to discuss the grievance. Both sides have a statutory right to be represented. The chairperson, who may be a senior manager from your own company or an outside conflict management specialist, should give everyone the opportunity to explain their side of the issues. Make any suggestions you may have for resolving it. After the meeting you should receive written notification to tell you what has been decided.

If you do not agree with the decision you should give notice to say that you are appealing against the decision, and explain why you do not agree with it. A further meeting to discuss your appeal should be arranged. Where it is possible, more senior people should deal with this appeal. Following this appeal meeting you should receive written notice to tell you the final decision.

As was mentioned earlier, this is a tortuous process, and you may still not be satisfied. In the pursuit of justice, however, if you are still not happy with the decision, you may want to consider other ways of resolving this grievance. Several options for dispute resolution are open to yourself and any of your people. But remember, the higher up this scale you go, the more difficult it becomes to solve the problem without rancour; probably the only solution is compromise, which is sometimes hard to swallow.

Options for resolving disciplinary and grievance matters

Mediation

The organisation may consider mediation as a way to help resolve the problem. Mediation is completely voluntary and confidential. It involves an independent, impartial person helping to reach a solution that is acceptable to everyone. The mediator may come from within the organisation or, if necessary, consider bringing in an external mediator. However, external mediation services are probably not free. If you agree to use outside mediation, also agree who covers the cost. If mediation is unsuccessful, all the other options are still open, so there is nothing to lose by trying it.

Conciliation

If there seems to be no alternative left to you but to go to an employment tribunal, a conciliation service may be able to help. This could find a way of settling the matter and avoid the need for an employment tribunal claim, which is the final step in what has become an intractable and costly process. Even if this step is taken, there can be no guarantee that both sides will be satisfied.

Employment tribunal

If other options for sorting out your problems at work have been exhausted, and you still do not feel your concerns have been satisfied, you may consider going to an employment tribunal. This is a challenging and stressful course of action. Consider very carefully. You may not get the results you want and the case could be very damaging to good working relations.

The ultimate course of action is termination. This may cost a lot in compensation, the final decision for which will be out of your hands. There is a high probability that the relationship between yourself and your people could be seriously damaged or at least changed by all this contention. You need to boost and maintain morale among your people.

Morale is something that animates the group. With good morale the group is enthused with a positive and successful spirit; relationships are cohesive and harmonious. Group members act in a way that strengthens wellbeing. All this comes from the way in which the group perceives they are being treated and the joint sense of doing something worthwhile.

With good morale comes positive discipline, where the group accepts control and direction at the expense of personal wishes and convenience. They are willing to do this for the team's sake. Individuals regulate themselves in the interest and wellbeing of the group or team.

Again, this happens because team members and the group as a whole feel that they are well treated, listened to and cared for. In working with people if you have created a good environment you will have little difficulty with discipline and grievance matters.

To summarise

Establishing morale is promoted by a management style which:

- establishes and maintains good lines of communication
- cares for its employees from all aspects, both personal and on the job
- has clear objectives that have been explained and can be understood by all
- lets people know what is expected of them, with good, clear job descriptions

- has rules which are fair and sensibly applied
- keeps people informed and involved in developments
- has good supervisors and middle managers
- gives constructive feedback and criticism
- makes training, development and career opportunities available to all.

Thinking about frustration

There will be times during your working life as a manager when you will be totally fed-up. This is, of course, not unusual whether in work or your private life: as you will have realised in reading this book there are plenty of opportunities in business for frustration, irritation and sheer annoyance. But it is not only the people you work with that will give you grief and some of these factors are identified in this quiz. Thinking about these factors may help to remove the resentments that you may sometimes feel towards your people. They are not always to blame! Very often the conditions of your work are not within your, or your people's, control; this will often give rise to tensions and agitation which could lead to conflict and possibly even disciplinary action. Remember it is not only your fault; it rarely is a single person who is responsible for unpleasantness in the workplace.

Considering some of these factors may shed light on some of the problems you may have encountered, and enable you to deal with the frustration caused in a calm and rational way. The commentary at the end will help you.

Here are some of the factors that tend to frustrate you in your managing role. These are not definitions, nor statements of depth, merely overall concepts to consider. Rank these ideas: 1 = high, 16 = low.

No.	Factors	Rank
1	Company policy	
2	Activities of higher managment	
3	Activities or inefficiencies of other sections of your organisation	
4	Paperwork and red tape in your organisation	
5	Trade union and/or staff council activity	
6	The fact that you have too much to do in too little time	
7	Poor physical working conditions and/or lack of equipment in your section	
8	Your own lack of technical knowledge and/or training	
9	Your own ability to handle people and/or communicate	
10	Your own lack of motivation and/or enthusiasm for your job	
11	The fact that some or all of your staff are awkward, lazy and disruptive, etc.	
12	Poor quality/low standards of ability of staff.	
13	Low pay for staff.	
14	Shortage of applicants for vacancies.	
15	Poor training facilities for staff.	
16	Poor selection and recruitment.	

Frustration commentary

The frustration factors fall into three broad categories: (1) your bosses; (2) your people and (3) yourself.

Items 1, 2, 3, 4 and 7 can essentially be seen as factors outside of your control and, insofar as they hamper you in doing your job, they are highly frustrating. You will probably have ranked one of these as your number 1, and very likely others as your 2 and 3. As far as item 7 is concerned, does the safety aspect worry you?

Items 5, 11, 12 and 16 relate to the people you work with. You will probably have ranked them from 5 to 9. They are irritations, but not totally out of your control; you can have some influence. At least you can say your piece and maybe motivate your staff a little. When thinking about items 12 to 16, consider what it is that makes for the low quality of your staff. Is there anything you can do about any of these things that will lessen your frustration level? You have probably ranked these items quite high. They are certainly important factors.

Items 6, 8, 9 and 10 of course concern you. And unless you are very honest with yourself, you have probably ranked most of them quite low, say from 9 to 16. Your own failures, in time management, motivational, communication and technical skills, frustrating though they are, are not your fault – or are they? You are probably right to rate them low down as frustration factors. But these problems are within your own hands to solve. Hopefully you will have gathered some ideas from this book that will help you sort out these areas of frustration.

SUMMARY

In this chapter we have considered some of the most difficult matters in dealing with people – discipline and grievances. Knowing the procedures and rules set up by your company reasonably well is helpful, but remember you also have colleagues with greater experience from whom to seek advice. There is also your HR department who will be skilled in these matters. In any dispute situation, it is essential to maintain excellent communications and you should try to be as empathetic as possible. Morale within any group involved in workplace tension will tend to be low. You need to bolster this using all the good management practices you can call on, because your team needs to have confidence in you.

But this confidence is often strained; there are many frustrations in all areas of the job of working with people. Some are obvious; others are more deep seated and difficult. You will need to learn how to diminish them to tolerable levels, or live with them and possibly have cause to leave.

How can you collaborate effectively?

Companies often grow haphazardly, with people and departments added on at random when they're needed. Has this happened to your company? Productivity may drop simply because people are not sure what to do and have no one they can ask for help.

What does your organisation look like?

The structure of an organisation will have a great influence on whether the investment made in training your people will be worthwhile or wasteful. The structure should be continually reviewed so as to anticipate developments in operating strategy. Successful organisations rarely stay static; they change. Change, properly planned and implemented, offers stimulation and opportunity. Effective communication in bringing about change emphasises the need for good collaboration in a fluid situation. Your people need to know and fully understand what is happening and where they, as individuals, stand in the current developments.

Different organisational structures and systems of management are needed to cope effectively with different environments and conditions. But there is no best way for organisations to be structured and organised. What you, in your own sphere of activity, must be is aware of what other departments are doing. You are not alone in your organisation and there is an emphatic need to collaborate with others who depend on your work, just as you depend on them.

Most organisations have a business strategy; they work to plans and budgets. Strategic aims and priorities are decided at the top, by the directors; they cannot delegate this overall responsibility. However, they have delegated to you the responsibility to manage your sphere of activity and, within that, to delegate certain functions. More about effective delegation will be found later in this chapter.

Your main function is to ensure operational efficiency supported by, as it were, good planned maintenance for people. This includes careful selection, effective training schemes, manpower planning and stable industrial relations. In today's climate there will undoubtedly be more strategic elements needed to link the organisation of your people with the future business environment.

Consulting staff

You have a very valuable resource working for and with you; make use of the extensive knowledge of all your people. Encouraging communication of ideas and opinions from your people to management is essential if you want full efficiency. At one end of the scale is a system of representatives and consultation committees, at the other is your local level team problem solving. Both types of consultation improve efficiency and, most importantly, increase the sense of involvement of your people.

Direct discussion between employees and management is always a good idea. Managers need to be aware of the attitudes and feelings of those who will be affected by management decisions. Without such discussions you will certainly make wrong decisions. Some system of committee meetings with elected representatives is necessary. This is not a waste of management time, but is an opportunity to increase efficiency and take a useful step forward in any participation policies.

The consultative committee does not put over management policy; that is the job of managers and is best done in team briefing. The purpose of this excellent example of collaborative working is:

- to give employees a chance to improve decisions by contributing comments before decisions are made
- to make the fullest possible use of their experience and ideas in the efficient running of the team's activities
- to give management and their people the opportunity to understand each other's views and objectives at first hand.

There should be no barriers to what such a committee can discuss, but certain matters such as trade secrets, personnel matters and union agreements will be off limits. Here are some examples of what can usefully be discussed:

- Outputs and productivity, such as improvements in work methods, office planning, central services, design of machines, transport, office equipment.
- Manpower policies and procedures, for example principles guiding promotions and transfers.
- Education and training, which could cover introduction of new members of the group, training of young people and retraining as needed.

- Health and safety matters, such as investigation of the causes of accidents.
- Selection and training of people for particular projects.
- Effectiveness of communication, within the group and between management and the group; how to improve this and what means to be used to do so.

The list could go on, but the main point is that collaboration is strengthened. Everyone concerned should feel that they can air their thoughts on the way the work of the group is carried on without worrying 'Have I said the wrong thing?' The feeling of all being on the same side is accepted.

Influencing people

In working with people we need to negotiate, and are almost under a compulsion to collaborate, to work together. We do this by the way in which we influence others, and how others influence us; we either get pulled or pushed. Either way the style you use to influence people is hugely important to the way you work with people. We will look at the 'pull' style first.

Pull influence style

Influencing involves personal disclosure, which means being assertive and admitting 'I have a problem'. Asking for help makes you seem vulnerable and gives you a reputation for honesty, authenticity and openness.

It also means involvement by generating a shared identity, and thus creating a fellow feeling. What you can also do is a sort of lobbying by creating a common objective, which gives people a feeling of togetherness and makes people willing to accept responsibility. Giving recognition and praise plus listening and paraphrasing gives the message to people that you are on their side; by showing exciting possibilities and being enthusiastic gives people confidence that you are sharing their hopes and visions.

The pull influencing style is highly motivational, which creates the situation where people want to do it. The individual reacts positively and the forces against change decrease. But beware: insincere pull styles are perceived as manipulative and dishonest, and will result in rejection. Nevertheless, well thought out Pull influence will be much more collaborative and gain you greater commitment and more effort, with higher quality but possibly slower and different results.

Push influence style

Push influence styles invoke an altogether different style of collaboration, one where people may feel repressed and unwilling to conform, or perform to set standards. This style of influencing seems to be forcing the other person to do something they would rather not do; it is moving not motivating them. It certainly builds up the forces against change. It also creates a WIN:LOSE situation, which may get you a quicker result or, on the other hand, no result at all.

You cannot use the push style and then try to use the pull style; it just won't work. People will become suspicious. There is a lot of logical reasoning for and against stating objectives, and reasons for the action required, and showing the problems of not doing it. The whole thing could become rather oppressive or even aggressive. This is the carrot and stick approach. We have to remember that people's wants are affected at least as much by their emotions and their need for controlling by themselves, as well as political factors. And people often reject rationality.

Using push influence you could easily slip into threatening or punishing behaviours, using your authority aggressively, or nagging, pressurising and being manipulative. This will result in people wanting revenge; they will have lost face because of your behaviour. To placate people you may then resort to bargaining or offering rewards or even bribery. The result is that people could feel insulted to be offered a reward. This may well become a right and be constantly increased to give the same performance level.

This may not be just money, but will probably include all sorts of other incentives. Push influence is a sort of self entrapment but it may have to be used occasionally; pull influence is much better for collaboration. Your skill in using these tools will judge your effectiveness as a manager.

Delegation

You are working with people all the time and, as there is no way that you can do, or supervise, everyone's job, you delegate. This can be formal or involve varying levels of informality. Good delegation is the best way to increase your efficiency. We know what delegation means, but we don't practise it as well as we could. Delegation is the closest form of collaboration that we can get. It is most efficient when performance of a task is entrusted to a person who can do the work and the expected results are understood by both parties.

Delegation extends your ability to manage the job; it is both an opportunity and a responsibility. Take great care in how you delegate and to whom you delegate. The right choice of jobs for delegation is essential, so is the right choice of person and their training. You need to understand all aspects of the job. Consider what is possible to delegate and what is not; there are some job elements and circumstances in which it would be unfair and irresponsible to delegate.

Remember too that whatever you delegate, the ultimate responsibility for the job remains yours; it is vital therefore that delegation, this most intimate of collaborative working, be done excellently.

To delegate efficiently we should:

- Choose the work to be delegated and choose the right person. The person selected should be able to do the job, but be prepared to guide and train if necessary.

- Define the job and ensure a clear understanding of what is expected. Outline the job, preferably in writing, discuss the objectives, agree the standards expected. Don't simply ask if they understand; all the pressure will be on them to say that they do understand. Instead, get them to explain what the job requires. Let them know that the channels of communication are open, that you will be available when needed, and that you have confidence in their ability to do the job.

- Prepare and motivate people. Build up their confidence, express your own confidence in their ability. Emphasise the importance of the delegated job. Say 'This is important, I'm entrusting you with it, I know you can handle it.'

- Supervise the work carefully but not too closely while they are doing the job. Encourage independence and upward communication (but not upward delegation!); show interest in their ideas, ask to be kept informed. Don't allow upward or reverse delegation to happen; time will be wasted and inefficiencies occur. If you waste time solving problems for other people (which they ought to be able to deal with themselves), you have delegated poorly. Similarly, you need to know your own problem solving and responsibility level without delegating upwards needlessly.

● Accept only completed work, a finished job that only
   needs your approval. You can't train people properly if
   you accept incomplete work; this creates inefficiency,
   they have to finish the job themselves.

The close working relationship that delegation involves, means we
have to decide what we can and should delegate, and what we
should not. Real consultation and good communication with the
people you delegate to will ensure success.
   You can and should delegate:

● routine tasks (and the responsibility and decision making
   associated with the task)
● complete jobs (gives a sense of achievement)
● jobs that others could do better (and possibly more
   cheaply).

Do not delegate:

● ultimate responsibility for the task
● tasks without guidance (tell them what you want done,
   and how it is to be done)
● unpleasant tasks (those are really your responsibility –
   you cannot offload them).

The delegation process

There are five distinct stages in the delegation process which move
progressively to you being able to devolve responsibility and
authority to the delegatee. Figure 11.1 shows the steady decrease
of your part of the job and the corresponding expansion of the
other person's job until full ownership is achieved by them.

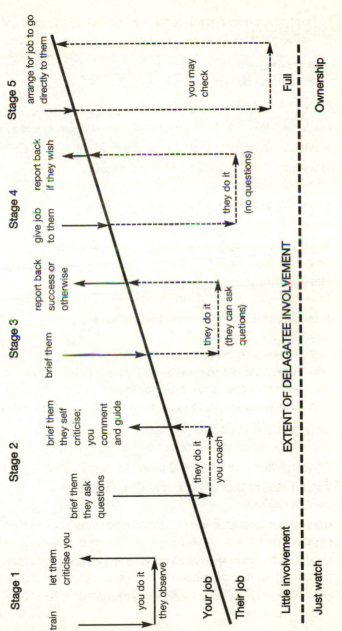

Figure 11.1 The delegation process

Delegation checklist

These are the matters you need to pay attention to when preparing for and actually delegating.

	No	Yes
Have you listed jobs that can be delegated?	☐	☐
Have you selected people who are capable, willing and interested?	☐	☐
Have you explained reasons for delegating?	☐	☐
Have you explained the results that you expect?	☐	☐
Have you relinquished authority – but maintained responsibility overall?	☐	☐
Have you let your people establish their own priorities – but you fix deadlines?	☐	☐
Have you followed up on the task? (Don't abandon the delegatees.)	☐	☐
Are you available for help when needed? (Invest time in explaining and coaching. This will pay off – but don't then do the job for them).	☐	☐
Do you demand finished work?	☐	☐
Do you refuse to accept problems? (But do encourage suggestions for solutions.)	☐	☐
Do you always give credit and praise for good work?	☐	☐
Do you believe that intelligent people learn from their mistakes?	☐	☐
Do you get feedback about the job from your people when it is complete?	☐	☐
Do you have training/coaching sessions during the job and after completion?		
Do you encourage your people to act as trainers for others?	☐	☐

These are all matters you have to think about. Consider your 'NOs' – is there room for improvement?

Assessing skills

One of your functions as a manager will be to do performance appraisals for your people; to assess their progress and deal with any areas of concern. This collaborative skill is very valuable because the interaction between manager and team is expanded to show real interest in the people with whom you work.

Appraising performance will include getting closer to understanding the individual to ensure they know what is required of them in their job, and know how they are succeeding in it. The process of talking to all of your people will enable you to know each of them better, and so identify how you can help them achieve more.

The appraisal process will enable you to jointly consider the personal history of the individual in relation to their job description, which should outline their function in the company. You should both review the training they have received and what the outcome of this has been in terms of past performance. You will be able to identify potential training needs and use the review to shape future performance targets.

This close interest in your people could certainly increase motivation and demonstrate your concern for the people you work with. You could expect your interest to stimulate and improve performance which will offer a good channel for feedback which will hopefully close the loop of group collaboration.

This is your opportunity to praise their successes and discuss, and maybe analyse, their problems and the causes. Also to find out what they enjoyed and did not enjoy, and why this was so.

Finally there are decision points as to where the person should be going, and what their own aims are in the short term. It is important to establish what help/training they need, and to set plans for this in motion to meet their own long-term aims. Encourage any other points for discussion that may arise; this can be very helpful in creating a trusting and collaborative relationship.

Getting to know your people in your own department, as well as those in other areas throughout the organisation, is an essential part of the job. We do not operate alone but are surrounded by others running their own sections with whom we need to cooperate. We will always need to negotiate with others and this is best done in a spirit of mutual understanding, which has been built up by getting to know the people with whom we work and collaborate.

Where we want to be

Every organisation will have a business strategy. This, however, may not be clearly defined and it is the responsibility of those organising it to develop strategic capability in the organisation, so as to bring on people who can think and act strategically. This is a serious part of management development.

Well-conceived business strategies will usually cover many areas: change in the organisation; more use of new technologies; introduction of new systems for operations and quality management; development of new products and services; improvements in customer service; and initiatives to attain employee commitment. Strategies concentrate on the future position of the organisation in its marketplace. Strategies cannot be implemented without the active collaboration of the people employed, not just from the managers but from the entire cadre.

This raises two questions: what is the contribution that we need from people to achieve our strategic outcomes; and how are we going to get this?

What do we need?

The next step is key: we need to express the organisation's business needs in terms of the people employed, their capability, performance, and the way they shape their contribution to the achievement of the business aims, remembering the economic environment and competitive strategy that has been decided upon.

But strategic aims, the outcomes of any organisation's plans can only be achieved when action is being taken to ensure that:

- the whole of the employed people are committed to the organisation's success and are competent to perform their present jobs well
- the senior management have the competence and capacity to establish well thought out directions and aims for the business so as to develop an organisation capable of achieving them
- all sections of the company can, and do, make a creative contribution to the organisation's success
- the organisation sustains people who are willing and able to meet the challenge of the future, whether this is anticipated or unexplained and unthinkable.

Opportunities and threats will arise. The organisation must be able to rely upon employees with varied interests, experience and achievements who have the habit of learning, and the skills and desire to learn; who have a broader competence than is needed just in their current jobs.

How shall we get what we need?

All this can happen only with good management practice and the encouragement from the management of people to learn and develop, so as to reach the planned outcomes. The creation of commitment is a vital strategic component in today's business environment and goes together with the level of competence throughout the organisation, plus its capacity for change. To support commitment everyone working in the business should, both as individuals and collectively, have a sense of belonging to the organisation. This is brought about by being informed, being involved and sharing success and having a sense of excitement in the job. Thus, in working with people, you can bring about through the creation of pride in their work, trust, and their own accountability for results. Have confidence in your management and leadership. This will come from your judicial exerting of authority, showing dedication and displaying competence. The example you set to your people is likely to be replicated in their standards of behaviour and performance.

The lead-up to all these desirable outcomes is contained in the chapters of this book. Not all will be attainable but, if at least some of the advice is followed, there will surely be significant improvements in worker/boss relationships, in productivity and, progressively, in a less stressful working environment.

SUMMARY

In this chapter we have touched on the structure of your organisation, how it has developed and what it will need to look like in the future.

The most suitable organisation structure for effective collaboration was also discussed, as well as the advisability of consulting with staff as widely as possible. Influencing styles that lead to good or poor collaboration, as well as the usefulness and importance of effective delegation in gaining sincere cooperation with your staff were outlined.

Finally your assessing and appraising skills were examined in the context of best practice management. The need to put the lessons argued in this book into operation were emphasised; if the desired outcomes, whatever they may be, are to be realised this will only happen if your manner of working with people is very skilful.

12

The Companion Interview: Digby, Lord Jones of Birmingham Kt on managing people, information and knowledge

The following interview with Lord Jones, when he was Skills Envoy for the UK in addition to holding a variety of non-executive and advisory roles (and before he received his peerage), was conducted by Ed Peppitt, author of *Six of the Best* (Hodder). Three years with the Royal Navy at the beginning of his working life taught Lord Jones about leadership, teamwork and the importance of constant communication. After qualifying as a solicitor he became a partner with Edge & Ellison before moving to KPMG and from 2000 to 2006 he served as Director-General of the CBI. In his interview Lord Jones focuses firmly on the importance of building great working relationships and team dynamics in his own career and in dealing with the increasing volume of knowledge and information in modern working life.

Ed Peppitt writes:

I had prepared for my meeting with Sir Digby Jones by researching and reading a range of interviews he had given with national and regional newspapers during his tenure as Director-General of the CBI. Whilst these made very interesting reading, they didn't provide the preparation I had hoped for. Described as 'like a very cuddly boxer' by The Sunday Telegraph, *and 'less Billy Bunter and more John Bull' by* Scotland on Sunday, *I desperately tried to build a mental picture of 'one of the most recognisable business faces in Britain'.*

However, the more I read, the more reassured I felt. I felt heartened to learn that we shared the same opinion about the BBC television programme 'The Apprentice'. In an interview with The Sunday Times, *he said: 'It puts business in a very bad light. Young people will be turned off because they think they will be shouted at by a horrible, fat, old, rich bloke.'*

Hardly one to mince his words, I was confident that if I asked straight questions, he would reward me with straight answers. It was a fantastic opportunity for me, but I was a little worried that I was discussing the subject of managing information and knowledge with him. Would he be stimulated by the subject matter? Would he have enough to say? Would we just spend an hour or two discussing IT systems?

In my mind, there were several issues that I think affect British business that I wanted to hear Sir Digby's opinion on. No one would deny that the amount of information passing an individual's desk each day has grown dramatically in recent years. What techniques or methods would he recommend for handling and managing information? For someone who has always been out and about, how has he personally managed to stay on top of the information he is required to absorb? Perhaps the two most important issues were about sharing knowledge between individuals and teams within an organisation, and also protecting that knowledge, and turning it into intellectual property.

I thought I would begin by asking him whether he recognised the Chartered Management Institute's quotation that, 'the amount of information produced and used by individuals and organisations continues to grow'.

The impact of the knowledge economy

I wanted to begin with a quotation from the Chartered Management Institute which says that, 'the amounts of information produced and used by individuals and organisations continues to grow'. Is that something you agree with?

Yes. It's on two levels, isn't it? Britain has made this shift with a considerable amount of pain and angst, and the journey is not finished by any means, but we are way ahead of any other country in Europe on this – I actually think we are ahead of America in this. We have made this shift towards a value-added, innovative, branded, quality economy for goods and services. We don't protect our markets, we don't put up tariffs and subsidies, we don't indulge in the hypocrisy of France and America, we just get on with it and we have restructured our economy. So that's why we don't dig coal out of the ground any more, that's why we don't make commodity steel, that's why we have the greatest and best financial services industry on earth. The reason is that we have moved to a value-added, innovative economy. You are always going to need people to do manual work; pick the fruit off the fields, do the labour on the building site, wait at table, chambermaids in hotels, all that sort of stuff, of course you are. But there are going to be no sustainable jobs for people without a skill of some sort within the next five years.

So the need for knowledge, the acquisition of knowledge, the handling of knowledge, the transmission of knowledge and information and the application of that to the wealth-creation process has never been more important and is an ongoing dynamic. Now at that level we are doing better than I think we ever thought we could. Of course, the big thing about a service-based economy is that it uses people. So we have got a low level of unemployment. We have got a hell of a lot of people who don't earn a lot of money, but they are in work. Those self-same people in Germany and France are part of their 11 or 12 per cent unemployment, and in France in the under 25s it is about 22 per cent, and this is because they haven't made this transition. So they haven't got this service-based economy where these people will work, albeit for low wages. So when people or trade unions say, we're a low paid economy – oh fine but they are in work. If they don't want them to have a job, albeit lowly paid, well no problem, we will go and do it in China. It's a shame they don't campaign for skills in the way they fight to keep yesterday's jobs.

So that is the one part of our knowledge. The other part is that the whole electronisation of our lives is predicated on the handling, transmission and acquisition of knowledge and information. Everything from the Internet to the mobile phone – the whole thing is predicated on that.

The impression I get from what you are saying is that the inevitable result in the transition is a swamping of knowledge for workers at all levels, as well as for managers and directors.

Oh yes. The upside of it is that without it we are dead. We are a globally engaged country, we trade like crazy, we are number one or two in the world in aviation, we are number one or two in the world in financial services, number one or two in the world in academia and pharmaceuticals. We are a class act, and we are still home to more different car makers than anywhere else on earth. Formula One employs 50,000 people in Britain, you know. Engineering, motor car engineering – top of the gang. Now all that stuff we are very, very good at. Creative industries – about 12 per cent of the world's creative industry's GDP we do in this country – art, video, advertising, design, architecture, music, film, all of those things.

What have I just described to you, if it's not the handling of information and knowledge? The downside – and this is, I think, one of the great challenges for managers, and a huge challenge in the public and private sectors at management level – is that there is *too much* information, and how do you sift it, how do you prioritise it, how do you become good at picking out the stuff you need and discarding the stuff you don't? How are you going to be skilled at prioritising? How do you handle the swamp, which can really depress people and move pressure to stress very quickly? How do you educate people to handle information better so they don't waste people's time with giving them too much information or unnecessary information? And then at the same time, there are two great things that authority does – be it regulators, be it for this purpose media, I mean anybody with a degree of influence and authority. First, they say, 'Right, you cc Fred on every email, so Fred is now deemed to have seen it, so if Fred does nothing about it and the shit hits the fan in five years' time well, you knew about it Fred'. So what do you do about that? Second, you have the whole issue of regulation and regulatory form-filling. Just try being a police officer trying to make an arrest … or a chief executive of a hospital.

The whole red tape issue.

The whole red tape issue is born out of enhanced information and a greater knowledge transfer. The ability to store it, the ability to deal with it, it is all born out of that, because it is easier to do, far more easy than it used to be.

Stress, pressure and the impact on individuals

Sir Digby Jones had highlighted several concerns that I wanted to investigate further. He had talked about the impact that IT has had on individuals, particularly in terms of the amount of information that has resulted. It might be convenient to copy a number of people in on emails, but the swamp of information that results is a concern. Then there is the issue of red tape. The notion is that regulation and form-filling has evolved because, with IT systems in place, it is so much easier to store the information, so you might as well collect it.

I wanted to ask Sir Digby his views on two separate, but related, concerns. First, I wanted to discuss the effect that the increase in information and knowledge has had on the average British worker. Does this increase explain the growing levels of stress and pressure in the British workforce and, if so, what is to be done about it? Second, for someone who, as Director-General of the CBI, was expected to have an incisive and up-to-date comment on just about anything, how does he decide what information is important and what is not? How does he prioritise his agenda? How does he keep on top?

As Director-General of the CBI, you always gave the impression in interviews, or when writing for newspapers, that you had a comment to make on virtually anything of value or noteworthy to business – and yet, by your own admission, you are always out visiting business, you are always travelling about. How do you personally decide what is relevant or important, and what is not?

Three things. One is, I delegate. I am a very, very good delegator. I do not employ clever people to work for and with me and then do the job myself. I have no problem in trusting them. Sometimes, being human, they let me down. But frankly you've got to trust them. And you give them the appropriate praise: if it is their idea or their piece of work, then you tell whoever reads it that it's their piece of work, and you surround yourself with clever people. So they then start being the interface for handling a lot of that information. For example, they sift my emails. When I first got the job seven years ago I did a speech in a hotel in Manchester and I was then in my hotel room and doing my emails on my laptop at two in the morning. It was ridiculous! So I said that's it, you guys can sift it, you can sort it, and you give me what is important so I can read it, and you deal with the rest. That system works. Was it 100 per cent foolproof? No. Am I prepared to carry the can if they let me down which in turn means that I've let somebody down? Yes, of course I am. That's why I'm paid to be the boss and that's why I'm appointed as the boss.

The second thing I do is, I read – I read prodigiously. I get driven around, I sit on airplanes, I sit on trains and I read. I read the *Times* and the *Financial Times* every day, the *Sunday Times* and the *Observer* on a Sunday – and as I go to bed at night, well thank God for satellite news and News24 or Sky News, every time of day or night I've got it, which is fabulous. When I am overseas I watch BBC World. I don't watch CNN because I don't want to know only what is happening in America, I want to know what is happening in the world through independent eyes! So I keep absolutely up to date on that.

Then the third thing is, and I am quite good at this, I am a ruthless prioritiser.

So the typical very well-rehearsed model of urgency and importance – if it's not urgent, or not important, it just gets chucked away?

Or it certainly waits its turn. I am very ruthless at managing myself.

Are you a speed reader?

Yes – and I have a very good memory.

Short- and long-term?

Yes. But I am not particularly IT-literate. I don't have a computer at all. I haven't got one at home. Pat and I do not have a computer in the house. I haven't got a laptop. I am a prodigious texter and a big user of mobiles, but I don't have a computer. Matt and Aimée are my two PAs – Matt's at Deloitte and Aimée is at BARCAP – and they do the lot. If you email me, it goes to Matt. I know how to use a computer, but I just don't have one. I go on the web by saying, 'Matt, go on the web'. Aimée does my research and project work.

So if you are in a hotel and there is a paper that Matt thinks you ought to read ...

He faxes it to me.

I'd like to come back to that, because I'd like to look at the impact that has on the stress and balance and staying in control.

I do take my holidays. I have six weeks' holiday a year and I always, always take them. I have taken them all through Edge & Ellison, all through KPMG, all through the CBI and now I still always take my holidays. In the CBI I probably rang in once a week and said, 'Is everything OK?', but I had a deputy – John Cridland – who was really good. And why do it myself on holiday if I have a damn good deputy?

It's the management of yourself, that's what's so important. Although I don't often work on Saturdays I do sometimes work for two or three hours on Sundays, in the afternoon or evening. For example, last night – I had a whole pile of work to do. Now because I'm a human being I found myself starting to do the easy things first. I even did some things which actually were not time-critical for today at all, but they were easy, so I had to force myself to move on to the more challenging things, which were time-critical for today. Handling the information is very important. If I have one problem with this, it is that I find it very difficult to say no. I'm not good at saying no – I like pleasing people and I like doing things for people.

And is it one of your PA Matt's roles ...

To rein me in? Yes! And he does as well.

You talk about having a good memory. Is that something you've always had or you've learned?

No I've always had it. For instance, I don't use notes when I speak. People say, oh it comes easy for you – it doesn't. I always get nervous before I speak, but I excuse myself over the coffee and I will go and sit in the loo, put the lid down and just for five minutes get my act together and just think, 'That's the order in which I want to talk about it, those are the facts I want to bring into it, that's where I want to leave the audience at the end of it'. I plan it every time. So although it looks like I just stand up and do it off the cuff, it's actually planned. But if it wasn't for my memory, I wouldn't be able to do that.

If I could give someone three things to succeed in twenty-first century Britain, the first one would be the use of your memory and the ability to handle knowledge – to handle the information that comes in, to remember things, to discard stuff and to exploit stuff.

So the first ingredient of success is a combination of prioritising and memory?

Yes, prioritising and memory, and the discipline of giving yourself time to do it.

The second thing would be confidence. But that comes with knowing you are feeling competent about what you are doing. You are then confident, and feel on top. You may be under pressure, but you are not under stress. Stress is pressure you cannot deal with. I will come back to that.

And the third thing, and there is no escape from this: you work very hard and there is no substitute for this. Twenty-first century developed economies face huge challenges and you can't escape the work ethic, full stop. It doesn't mean that you don't make time to go and see your kid at his speech day, it doesn't mean that you don't get home and take your wife to the theatre – it is just a question of handling your time and working hard.

It sounds to me, from what you are saying, as if you don't suffer stress because you have got the balance between work and your life outside work?

Yes. I'll give you an example. Pat and I have just been away for a month. Between the two jobs, I did a month of quite a lot of speeches and TV and other things, I did a month of being briefed on all these jobs I'm now doing, and then I had a month off, and we went away on a three-week cruise around the Black Sea and then a week in Australia. We got back last Monday. And I'm a big 'Spooks' fan – and I taped those four episodes for the four weeks that I missed. And yesterday I said to Pat, 'I am going to curl up on the sofa and I'm going to watch all four!' Now, I've got a whole pile of work to do and I've got calls to return and all sorts, but I promised myself I was going to do it, and my time is important to me, and *I* matter to me. So I did it.

You see, many people say, 'I haven't got time to do that because I've got to do all this work'. Well fine, but you must put some balance in your life. Pressure is fine, stress is not. I know what stress is like. I can remember in 1997 I was senior partner of the law firm Edge & Ellison, and I had a great time, loved it and all that, I was very young to be doing the job and I wanted the firm to go down a particular path, and frankly they wouldn't. I tried to cajole them, I tried to push them, and at the end of the day the only thing I was left with was saying, 'If you don't, I'm leaving'. And I was not in control of events. I had got to the point where I had shot the hostage, actually. So I handled it badly and I basically said, 'I'm going'. Now, I was under pressure, but I couldn't control events. Other people were controlling events, not me. The timetable, what happened next – I was entirely reactive, I wasn't in charge of the agenda, I wasn't even contributing to the agenda. Those were three of the unhappiest months of my life. The level of pressure was no different, it really wasn't. The fact was, I had no control over it, and I know I was under stress. Pat and I don't row, but I was certainly horrible to be with during that time. I drank too much. I ate too much. I didn't exercise enough. I had all the classic symptoms of being under stress. I don't smoke, but if I did I would probably have been on 80 a day. I don't do drugs, but if I did I was probably going to be mainlining or something! For me this was a bad time, although others may have thought that there was nothing much wrong. It was only for about three months, but it was hard. There was one Sunday morning, a glorious autumn day, I was down at the bottom of the garden on the bench reading *The Sunday Times* and Pat came along with a mug of coffee, and she tripped and dropped the coffee on my paper. I went absolutely wild! And she stood there and said 'What on earth …? The newsagent is 300 yards away and it's only £1.25!' And I remember looking up at her and saying, 'What's happening to me?' And it was because I was not in charge of events.

So, the next day I walked into the office and said, 'That's it, I'm going'. I told the partners privately that I was leaving and we planned a way of working me out of the firm. I was back in control. Life was very difficult then with lots of pressure, but so what! It was *pressure*, it wasn't *stress*. There was a difference, I could see it, and I have never forgotten.

That's very interesting, I've never looked at stress and pressure in those terms before. When I feel stressed I tend to take it out on my kids.

And that is because you have shifted from being in charge. You can be under enormous pressure, but if you are in charge of your own involvement in it to the point where you might want to say, 'I'm going', then you are in charge of it. When you lose control of your space, and somebody is running you, and you are reacting, you will do negative things: you will eat too much, drink too much, take it out on the kids, take it out on the missus – you will do something negative or destructive, because you are no longer in charge of events. In an information society it gets even worse because you walk in to the office and there are 47 emails, all with 'cc Digby Jones'.

Absolutely. So the picture I am getting is that you are blessed in many ways because you have a very good memory, you are good at prioritising and you are good at delegating – and these are all pretty essential skills.

And I monitor it myself.

Talk me through that.

I have a little expression which I often say to myself, and certainly I say it to my PAs Matt and Aimée sometimes and my wife Pat at other times: I say it's 'not my finest moment', which means that I know I could have done better. I have no problem in knowing when I was very good and I also know when I could have done it better. I sit and analyse how I could have done it better.

So you learn for next time?

Yes you do. I do that. I sit down and I think, now where and how could that have been better? And sometimes nothing you did could have made it better, but sometimes it could. And sometimes it's that you've got away with it. I know I have sometimes winged it, I have come away and thought 'Thank God for that', when actually I wasn't fully equipped with the information and everything else, but I got away with it. But always be honest with yourself.

One of the other things I do is, I always read my brief. Always. Because in my job I used to see politicians who hadn't read their brief, and it was pathetic to see. So I've always read my brief. Even if it means I'm ten minutes late because I'm sitting in the car reading it before I walk in, I always do it. Fortunately, because you are often travelling you can read your brief on the hoof. But read the information, analyse it, be prepared.

Communication

I found Sir Digby Jones's distinction between pressure and stress both fascinating and, from a personal perspective, very useful. However, I wanted to look in more detail at the principles of 'priority' and 'memory'. I have no doubt that both are vital in the effort to manage information. However, I have known a few corporate lawyers in my time, and I have witnessed the reading and assimilation that they have to do to prepare for a case – the paperwork alone is often measured by the box. I wondered whether the corporate lawyer relies on other tools and techniques to stay on top? Having been a corporate lawyer himself for almost a decade, I wondered how Sir Digby had coped.

I'd like to ask about your time at the law firm Edge & Ellison. I once worked for a company which bought another company, and the paperwork involved was immense. There were three directors

in this publishing company, and we all spent many weeks reading the papers. I didn't feel that I had any control over it at all. Then a corporate lawyer came in to advise us, went through the paperwork in probably about 25 minutes, and already knew more about what was going on than I did. Is that just memory? What skills are involved there? You must have been involved with these sorts of things time and time again?

Oh yes. The one thing that corporate lawyer had wasn't the knowledge he possessed of the deal, it was his ability to communicate it to you. He obviously had the ability to distil the knowledge, handle it, and then communicate it to you because the one thing we haven't talked about, and perhaps we should now, is this ability. You can have all the information in the world, you can prioritise yourself, but if you can't communicate it you are dead. And he obviously had the ability to take all this information and say, 'Let me simplify it for you'. He wouldn't be patronising you, but he would simplify it for you, and he would make it easy to understand.

He was talking my language?

Yes. That's what a good lawyer does. It is a skill. Can you learn it? Yes, you can become a better communicator. Are you born that way? Yes you probably are actually. My old Housemaster at Bromsgrove (who sadly died in September) always used to tell this story, whenever I went back for Old Boy Days. He taught Biology and he said, 'I can remember one day explaining something in Biology at O level, and this guy at the front of the class was sitting there, and he was finding it very, very difficult, and I looked up, and you were at the back of the class talking to your mate and looking out of the window. And when I'd finished explaining it I said, "Right Jones, maybe you might like to talk us through it".' Then he said, 'What really pissed me off was that you came to the front of the class, and you did it! And what was worse, the bloke at the front said after that, "Oh I understand it now sir!"'

That's a lovely story. But I bet the chap you were chatting to at the back didn't get it!

No, he wouldn't have got it – he probably failed his Biology O level. And it's the ability to explain it in words that people understand, because you get no prizes for showing somebody you are really clever if they haven't understood it. It is very important.

So maybe it's not just assimilating the knowledge, but it is also being able to communicate it – interpret it and then communicate it?

Yes, and it's also important to look at how you handle the information. I mean it's that old cliché, isn't it – 'I'm sorry this letter's so long, I didn't have time to write a short one'.

I'm a copywriter, so I face that all the time!

It's your job, isn't it, to distil it down. I did an article before I went on holiday and they wanted 400 words on a particular subject, and I wrote down all my thoughts, and when I counted it up it was 1,800 words, and the skill was to get that to 400 without losing the flavour of the article. That took an ocean of time.

Writing down 1,800 words, just dumping my thoughts, that was straightforward. I'd like to think they were rather good thoughts, but it was not the most difficult thing in the world to do. The difficult thing was to hone it to 400. Now that is the ability to communicate efficiently and it is very, very important.

People are kind enough to say things to me like, 'You were on Radio 4 and in one minute I understood the issue'. I didn't have any training for it. I arrived at the CBI and they said, 'Right, we are going to send you on media training', and I said, 'What for?' And they said, 'Well you've never had any'. I said, 'I have been recruited to be me, and I'm a quick learner, I'll make loads of mistakes, but I am going to be me.'

That is very interesting. When I was talking to Andy Green, he said that he had had all sorts of problems when he first stood up to talk or present, until his trainer said that he should just stand up and be himself. After that, he said, he found it very much easier.

Yes – I mean, if you stand up and be you, what you've then got to learn to do is to fine-tune yourself, but you haven't got to try to be someone else, and there's a big difference. You know, people say to me, 'We've asked you for a 30-minute speech, not a 40-minute speech'. Now all I've got to do is distil me, or to get my feelings into a one-minute interview with John Humphrys. I am still me, I've just got to look after me, whereas if somebody says, 'Right, well you are not going to be you, you are going to be a different sort of person', then you'll get found out. They'll have you – interviewers such as Jeremy Paxman or John Humphrys will eat you for breakfast!

Well I was going to say that there must be times when you're glad that you've got some self-confidence ...

Well, that grows over time.

The long hours culture

Although I felt armed with some very practical techniques for managing information personally, I still felt that organisations have been slow to react to the amount of information that their employees are obliged to manage. There is a need for organisations to create a culture where knowledge is shared between people and teams on a systematic basis. I wondered if the long hours culture was another by-product of the information age, and whether Sir Digby Jones was a supporter of it.

I've worked in so many organisations where the culture is, that if you are not in at eight in the morning, and if you are leaving the office before half past seven at night, then you are obviously not doing your job properly. Is the long hours culture something that irritates you?

Actually no. I'm a long hours guy. I am trying to be very honest with myself here. When I was at Edge & Ellison and I was clambering up the greasy pole I would get in for about half-seven in the morning, and if we weren't going out to a dinner or something I would leave at about half-seven at night. As I started to build a team, and be in charge of a team, I don't think I ever said to somebody, 'I'm expecting you to stay late', but they did anyway.

Why?

Because the boss did. And I would be lying to you if I hadn't. It would be the easiest thing in the world now to say to you, well you know they are barmy if they work long hours. What I did do though, to be fair, is I'd say to somebody, 'Nothing you are doing now cannot wait until tomorrow, so you are not impressing me by doing it now. Go home'. Or, 'You've got your kids' sports day or something, go and do it'. But if it had to be done for tomorrow, oh yes, I expected them to work through the night, and I really did expect it. And at the CBI I used to call my first meeting 'morning prayers' and I used to have all my close people together at nine o'clock Monday morning but always held my first meeting in the office an hour before that.

OK, setting the tone for the week ...

Yes, so my wife and I used to leave our house in Warwick on a Sunday night at about ten o'clock, get to London at about half-eleven, go to bed, get up refreshed and ready to call my first meeting at eight o'clock Monday morning, so you start bang, eight o'clock Monday morning. I make no apology for that because, as I said earlier on, there is no substitute for hard work. That does mean you put the hours in. But you see, working harder doesn't mean working more hours, it means applying yourself, possibly exhausting yourself, but doing it within that time-frame. It was half-seven when Matt and I left here the other night because something had to be done for the next day, and frankly, I have no idea what time he is going tonight but if he's not out of here at five I'll be amazed. It is not my problem ... just get the work done.

So it's in line with necessity?

Absolutely, it's in line with necessity. The long hours culture is where people stay because it is the ethos of the place to work long hours. It ought to be a results-based culture. Now in a results-based culture you probably have to work long hours, but not all the time, and you probably have to work hard, but you are driven by performance. I give A for achievement, not E for effort, that's a given.

OK, what I am hearing, though, is that whatever time of night it is, you get home, you shut your door and that is the end ...

Yes, that is the end.

Until the next day, or the next week, or until you're back from holiday, or whenever it might be?

Yes. When I was in corporate law I used to do the through-the-night big completion meetings; I knew one completion meeting that went on for three days – you would be in over the weekend doing it. When I was at the CBI I would do a speech after dinner most nights or I'd be travelling most nights. I work the evenings in the week, and people always used to say to me, 'God, you work hard', and I used to say, 'Nowhere near as hard as I used to work at Edge & Ellison!' I would get into bed about 11-ish, and the alarm would go at half-five in the morning. I've only ever needed between five-and-a-half and six hours' sleep a night, all my life – I can't remember the last time I had seven hours' sleep. Even as a kid, my mum says I never stayed asleep for long. And I sleep like the dead!

When I checked out of a hotel the other week they said, 'Sorry about the fire alarm last night', and I said 'What fire alarm?' I hadn't even heard it! I sleep really well. I have never taken anything to help me sleep, I have never taken a pill in my life. I sleep on planes. I slept when my first wife left me! I sleep when I've got a big, big deal the next day. Even when I've messed something up and I'm going to get a bollocking the next day, I still sleep!

That sounds like a pretty essential skill.

Yes, I think it is. Harold Wilson once said, didn't he, that he always slept well. And Margaret Thatcher has said that she always sleeps well.

Have you always set goals? Have you always had an end in mind, or a target in mind? Clearly when you were 20 you didn't think, 'In 15 years I am going to be Director-General of the CBI' I'm sure, but did you think, 'I'm going to be a hot-shot corporate lawyer'?

Yes.

At what stage did you know that?

When I joined Edge & Ellison I was 23 and an articled clerk, now called a trainee, and my ambition was to be senior partner. I was going to be senior partner, and I wanted to be the youngest senior partner, and I did it. But when I was Director-General of the CBI my ambition was to change the organisation and make a difference. I couldn't become Senior Director-General!

But there was an achievement in mind?

Oh yes, it was to increase the membership, to increase the public profile and to get the spirit going internally.

One of the things I expect that I will find quite challenging now is that, for the first time since I was 25, I am performing a role in which I have no executive responsibilities at all! I am an adviser. I am going to find this very strange but it is just one more challenge to meet and overcome.

I am sure that I am not alone when I say that I have worked for companies where employees hoard knowledge, regarding it as a way to protect their position. What can an organisation do about that? Worse still is when those same employees then resign, taking that knowledge with them to a rival organisation. Again, what can be done? I remember in my first job as a shop assistant in Stanfords, the map and travel bookshop in Covent Garden in London, there were three employees who survived in that store for ten years only because they knew so much about the stock they sold. They wouldn't have survived in any other business. Yet no one dared to get rid of them.

Quite. I remember at Edge & Ellison we had one partner – a brilliant lawyer – and he would say, 'Only I can do this'. Why? 'Well I'm the only one who knows it.' Well why don't you share that with someone else and they could do it? 'Oh no, no, no, no, no.' And you could just see that what he'd got stamped on his forehead was *insecure*.

So in your CBI days, what would you have advised particularly smaller organisations to do?

I used to say, you have got to move out of commodities, those goods and services that sell only on price. You have got to get into knowledge-based innovation. You must invest in kit and in people.

Kit as in IT?

IT – yes. And then what you must do is sell that knowledge to the world at value added prices.

OK, and what should they do internally?

Internally it's unrelenting isn't it? It comes from the top of the business. I've always maintained that people work for you and in your business through 'QED'. And it's in that order: The Q is the *quality* of what you do. The quality of the work that people are provided to do. The quality that is the reputational issue of the business.

The E is the *environment* in which you work. Is it a friendly place to be? Do people have a laugh? That comes from the top. I've always thought a little bit of teasing, nicely done, obviously not bullying (if you see a bully, sack him!), but a bit of teasing, a bit of joshing – Monday morning, your football team, all that sort of stuff – is healthy. And when I read women writing this stuff about, 'Oh it's dreadful in our office, they all talk about football'. Well of course they talk about football – they are human beings! You know, if you met two women at the water-cooler you'd talk about whatever women want to talk about – it might be football or it might not! Nothing wrong with it! And if you get that spirit of the environment in which you work right, then you do begin to break down those barriers of me, me, I, I.

At the CBI I used to have my door open always, and I always used to make sure people understood when I had forgotten to do something. So I used to shout out to Matt who was outside something like, 'Oh God, I'm sorry, I forgot!' And I used to make sure people heard me say it, because if they hear you say it they might become brave enough to say it themselves. And then I used to say to someone down the corridor, 'Can you do me a big favour, I'm not good enough at this, I don't understand this, you do. Could you do it?' And I remember one day, Matt rang me when I was in the car and he said there are two ways to get you to your next appointment – one is to get back in the Daimler and be driven around, but actually if you walk up that alleyway and turn right up the steps you'll be there. I said, 'OK I'll walk'. And he said, and I heard him do it, he said – 'Everybody be quiet, the Director-General is walking. The Director-General is walking – stop the presses!' And I thought: I've won this because they were teasing me, they were doing it with quite a bit of affection in their voice, they were admitting that we had created a good environment.

Then the third thing is D, it's the *dosh*. The money has got to be right. You can persuade people to work for less but you can't persuade people to work for a lot less. They have to have the dosh – they have to be able to pay the mortgage, go home at nights. One of the universal standards of appreciation is money. I've never understood why somebody wants a million when they have already got a million. I've never understood that because I don't want to die wealthy, I want to die fulfilled and happy. But we live in a free society and I am delighted the world's best talent want to work and be paid here rather than anywhere else. If you don't pay people the going rate they will feel you don't appreciate them and vote with their feet.

A friend of mine who is a multi-millionaire – and I don't know whether it's his phrase or whether he read it in a book – he says, 'Don't pay the going rate, pay the staying rate'.

Very real.

Just picking up on the idea of sharing knowledge between workers at all levels in an organisation, do you think that has almost created and caused the growth of CRM (customer relationship management) systems, for example?

Yes I do. There are two sorts of knowledge, aren't there? There's the keeping people constantly aware of their working environment, what's going on, using knowledge and information dissemination to get people to feel they belong and to get people just reacting as human beings. Then there's the second part of knowledge dissemination, which is what they need to do their job. There's the technical professional information they need, and in that the manager has to help the recipient of the knowledge by not just sending everything, but just sending what they need and probably sending a little bit more than they need, but not everything. You know, the easiest thing in the world is just to dump 40 pages, whereas actually they probably only needed a summary. But it is very important, and that's the manager's call.

And the cc on the email is another example?

It's a very good example. As I have climbed up the tree I find this often: managers taking responsibility for things they don't even know are happening, and nor *should* they know are happening.

When journalists write, 'Why didn't so-and-so know what was going on?', well – get real! He's running 40,000 people and God knows how many offices – get real! Life's not like that. Take responsibility for it, definitely, that's why you're the boss, but to be expected to know it all – not a chance.

Very interesting indeed. Just talking about the fact that in the knowledge-economy, using your definition, we have got people who feel more confident – feel more empowered, frankly – to move to another organisation that might be offering something more appealing. What measures can an organisation put in place to try to prevent that happening?

Well there is a danger of course, because the one problem with moving to a knowledge-based economy is that when your assets go home at six o'clock at night, when they actually walk down the road to another job, they take all the knowledge with them as well, and it is pointless saying, 'Well I won't skill these people because when I've skilled them they will leave me'. You know, welcome to life.

So it is QED again?

It's QED. And by the way, some you are going to lose. You are going to train them and they are going to leave. But there are going to be others that someone else has trained that you're going to get. So the dynamic has changed about how you recruit, what you look for and how win or you lose. I saw this change at Edge & Ellison. I can remember when I was head of the department, if we lost one of our lawyers it was as if the world had ended. What had we done wrong? By the end of it when I was Senior Partner you'd be losing some every month and you'd be winning some every month. The world has changed in that respect.

So what can you do to keep them? QED. And you want them to take pride in what they do and where and how they do it. The other thing you do of course, is you have got to succeed as a business because people will stay with a successful business. The other important thing you have to do – and this is more relevant to customer bases – is to make sure they understand that if they walk out of the door they don't take the customer list with them, and if they do you will sue them.

So you need those measures in place.

You do, and you need your people to understand that you will do it. You know, if you are approached by someone else who says, 'Come and bring your client base, bring your information', well you can come and bring the stuff that's in your mind. But don't put the rest on a DVD and take it out of the building – if you do, we will sue you.

And there are enough protection measures and contracts and the like to make that possible?

Yes. That's the other point isn't it? You have got to set out the football pitch on which you're playing and where the goalposts are. You have got to say, 'There are some rules here'.

At the CBI I used to tell my people: 'If you come and tell me you have made a mistake, it is then my problem, not yours. You've done the thing you should do. You have admitted you've made a mistake. I am now there to help you and to help the organisation sort it out. And you will usually find there is nothing new in this world and someone, somewhere in this organisation will have made precisely that mistake in the past – there's a way of getting out of it 90 per cent of the time. But if you lie to me, I shall sack you because it is not fair on me, or the team that trusts each other. But if you are prepared to come and tell me you've made a mistake, fine, although I'd rather you hadn't made it, and if you are making too many of them we might have to have a conversation about life, but you will never get shouted at, you will never get bollocked, and you will certainly more than likely go up in my estimation.' I really used to say that – and it worked.

And people knew that you meant that.

People knew it! And they respond to it.

I am sure they do! And of course the last bit was the important bit. If somebody did actually lie to you and you said, 'Well, take it as a warning', then presumably you lose that sense of credibility?

I can remember somebody came to work for me on secondment from one of the big firms of accountants, and I said all that to her. On about the third day I said, 'By the way, where's that thing you were going to do for me?' And she said that she had done half of it. So I said, 'Great, can I see what you've done? Let me see how far you've got'. She replied, 'Well it's only in rough'. So I said, 'That's OK, I just want to see it'. Eventually I said, 'You haven't done it at all, have you?' And she said no. I said 'Good, because if you'd said yes you would be going back where you came from'. I said, 'Well done, now I suggest you do it'. What was she going to try to do? She was going to try and tell me what she thought I wanted to hear, instead of telling me the truth.

You've just made me swallow because I've been guilty of that ...

Well we all have! I do it, we all do it, don't we? We are all human beings again. But this is something else in an information age that we have to be careful of. I don't know the answer to this, but people will tell you, write to you, send you, what they really legitimately, and honestly, sincerely believe is the truth. It happens to be erroneous. Something happened last week and I tell you, I would have gone in a witness box on oath and said X was X. Factually X was Y. I actually said to somebody, 'Oh it's so-and-so', and I really genuinely believed it, I wasn't lying. It happened not to be accurate. It was true as I saw it, but it wasn't accurate.

And that's an inevitable result of the age we live in?

It is, it's the age we live in. It's an inevitable result of it really, because everybody, from me to the taxi driver, is keeping more balls in the air than they have ever done before.

The impact of IT

I was aware that we had yet to discuss in detail the impact of IT on the information and knowledge economy. I knew that Sir Digby Jones was not a huge user of IT himself, but as Director-General of the CBI, he must have seen first-hand the impact and influence that it was having on industry and the workplace.

I asked him if he thought that we focus too much on the systems – the hardware and the software – to interpret information, rather than on the information itself. In the knowledge economy, is the reliance on IT essential?

It is essential, because that is your portal into being able to make the decisions, prioritise, discard, concentrate, focus. You have got to have those systems to download and dump information into you. You've got to. The problem is, where are your gatekeepers? What sort of world are you going to live in? Are you going to deal with all this? Is your PA? Are you going to have screening? What are you going to do?

It is interesting, isn't it, that the three things that are the real spur to consumerism's handling of information are football, pop music and porn, and those three things are really the mainstay of the consumerist IT revolution. Now what we've got to do is enable the profit to be made to invest the money to get even better, and at the same time ensure that society is protected a little bit from itself, and also ensure that we train people to handle the information and the knowledge. That's the answer. There is a little bit of 'ban it', but really you've got to train people to handle it.

Certainly the impression I get is that in earlier stages of the development of this knowledge economy we were very good as a nation at installing very sophisticated databases and other technology to store data without really giving any thought to what really needs to be retrieved and how to interpret what needs to be retrieved. Is that still true, or was that never true?

Oh yes, I think it is true. I'll give a very good example. My wife Pat's great-auntie died recently, and we are sorting out her estate. So we wrote to her gas supplier to say that Mrs Thompson has died, may we have a final account? And we get one, no problem, and they addressed it to the executors of 'Mrs Thompson deceased', fine, done. So can you explain to me why on Friday we got a letter from the same gas supplier addressed to 'Mrs Thompson deceased', asking if she would like to buy winter cover against a faulty boiler?! And I really did do this – I rang up the number, pressed one, pressed three, pressed seven, waited an age and finally got through and I said, 'Somebody typed that in. I am not going to blame technology because a human being typed that into a database. A human being did it, and they must therefore have typed in the word "deceased". Has it crossed your mind that that means this woman is dead?' Now there's no excuse for that. That is a human being issue. I don't like it when I have to press one, press three, press seven, wait, get told 'Your call is important to us' but I'm still going to make you wait. I fully understand that if I don't want to pay huge bank charges every month, as someone with a pension fund that's got shares in banks, I understand why I need to make a profit and all of that, but when the human being element lets itself down, then we can't hide behind technology. The human element in a knowledge-based economy is enormously important and we're not very good at that. And in that we have become worse.

Yes, inevitably. You may have waited longer for a reply 15 years ago but when you got a reply, it would be personalised and it mattered.

Absolutely right.

The legacy

Finally, can I just read you a quote of yours, shortly before you left the CBI? You said:

> 'To whoever takes the job, I would say that they have to get out and about. I spend two days a week travelling, talking to people. Also you have to do the work. You have to read the briefs, otherwise you get caught out.'

Is that the best tip to pass on to your successor?

The best tip is, if you are going to make a difference you have got to be able to lobby those who make the rules. By and large, these are politicians, and the route to public approval of what you are saying is the media. You are going to impress both the media and the politicians far more if you know what you're talking about. To be able to say to them, 'I was in Newcastle last week and I found that X, Y and Z', or 'I was in a school in Somerset and the Head Teacher said to me X, Y and Z' – then they listen, because it's real stuff. The greatest way of doing the job well is to get out and about. And sometimes, you don't want to. Waking up on a very wet, dull, grey Friday morning in a strange place isn't really my idea of fun, but it arms you with the essential tool to do the job. And what is it? It's people.

True, you've got to be bright, and you've got to read the briefs. But if you go out and visit a business in Nottingham and then do an interview with the local newspaper, then people like Mervyn King or Gordon Brown will take more note of what you say. Ultimately, you'll have a greater effect on society and you will do your job better, and make more of a difference and isn't that why we're here? To maximise the talents we are lucky enough to have to make a difference for the better.

Conclusions and recommendations

I remember reading in a newspaper article that Deloitte were delighted to secure Sir Digby Jones's services, not because of his experience as Director-General of the CBI, but because 'he's a bloody good businessman'. He certainly comes across as someone that you'd like to do business with. I'm quite sure he would be a tough negotiator, but there would be nothing underhand in his actions. He is straight talking, honest and exceedingly good company.

He has certainly mastered the art of managing himself. He will work long hours when necessary, and has done throughout his career. But he will take every holiday day he is owed, and when he gets home, his working day is done. He would certainly acknowledge that he has the balance between his work and home life under control. He is blessed with a very good memory, and he is a fast reader, both of which help him to keep on top of his workload, and to manage the information that passes his desk. He delegates responsibly, and looks back and learns lessons from things he could have done better. He has learned from experience the importance of prioritising his workload. Put these together, and the result is someone who seems always briefed, and always prepared. I was interested to learn that he would rather be ten minutes late, and prepared, than to arrive on time having not prepared properly.

In the twenty-first century, the biggest inhibitor of effectiveness and creativity in the workplace is stress. Sir Digby draws a key distinction between stress and pressure. We all face pressure, and must learn to accept it and deal with it. But stress is pressure over which we have no control, and that is the killer. We must get back the control in order for the stress to dissipate. His own experience of the effect that stress had on him certainly struck a chord with me.

It was refreshing to hear that protecting and sharing an organisation's knowledge, and turning it into intellectual property, is no easy task. You can ring-fence and patent what you have as much as you like, but sometimes the best route for an organisation is to accept that it can run with an idea for a good six months before it is stolen and copied. And those are the words of a corporate lawyer!

What of encouraging people to share the knowledge that they have, for the betterment of the organisation as a whole? Again, Sir Digby argues, this is harder than it sounds. People who retain knowledge, and refuse to share it, are often insecure. The answer is to create a 'QED' culture: People feel secure and empowered by the *Quality* of the work that they do, and the *quality* of the organization's culture. They are driven by the *Environment* in which they work, and also by the *Dosh* that you offer them. If you can provide QED, and your staff still won't share their knowledge within the organisation, then it's time for them to go.

It is very hard not to like Sir Digby Jones. He is interesting to listen to, and seems genuinely interested in what you have to say. He is straight talking, and his advice is highly practical and down to earth. He doesn't have all the answers, and he is perfectly prepared to say so. When I thanked him for sparing the time to talk to me, he said that he had thoroughly enjoyed every minute. What was so refreshing, was that he clearly meant it. And do you know what? I enjoyed every minute too.

Managing information and knowledge checklist

If you are looking for ways to manage the information and knowledge in your organisation, here are some issues to think about. You might want to find a few, valuable minutes to take a clean sheet of paper and jot down any ideas that the following list generates.

The impact of knowledge

'Without it, we are dead' (Sir Digby Jones). So what are you doing about it? How do you sift through information to identify what is important and what's not? How do you prioritise, and how could you prioritise more effectively? What measures could you introduce to educate your people how to handle information better? Could you delegate more? Could you delegate more effectively?

Habits

Do you copy people into emails unnecessarily? Why do you do it? Is it absolutely necessary? Are there procedures in your organisation that create red tape? Are they necessary? How could you simplify them? Could you get rid of them altogether?

Yourself

How effectively do you manage yourself? How good is your memory? Could you improve it? How? Do you find yourself 'winging it' when presenting or attending meetings? Would you be more effective if you were late, but prepared? Are you able to look back and admit that something 'was not your finest hour'? Do you analyse what you might have done better?

Stress and pressure

Do you agree that stress is pressure that is beyond your control? Are you under pressure or under stress? Looking at the stress in your role, what can you do right now to claw back control of the situation? Will you actually do it? Do you work long hours? If so, why do you? Does your organisation have a 'long hours culture'? What has caused it? Do you take your full holiday entitlement? Do you work at weekends and in the evenings? How well do you sleep? What changes are you going to make?

Protecting and sharing knowledge

What can you do to protect the knowledge invested in your people, and turn it into intellectual property? Are there legal steps you could take to protect your intellectual property? Are they worth it? Are you better off accepting that your competitive advantage won't last indefinitely? Do your people share the knowledge that they have? If not, is it because of insecurity? What measures could you introduce to encourage sharing of knowledge? How does your organisation rate in terms of 'QED' (quality, environment, dosh)? What role does IT play in storing data for creating shared knowledge?

Conclusion

This book has dealt with the tricky subject of working with people in a work context. There are many facets surrounding this subject and they all concern the art and science of management. The science concerns the operational techniques of managing; the art is about the people involved in the manager's job.

There has always been management, from the earliest times when a group of people gathered to get something done. There has to be some plan, some organisation, some Leader, so that what is to be done gets done. Modern management has evolved over the last couple of centuries into a fairly formal structure with a hierarchy of bosses and workers. The larger that businesses have grown, the wider the gap has become between the bosses and workers. This format generated real problems in getting things done with ever more rigid structures and less and less regard for the people who were doing the job. Gradually, over the last few decades, the form of management has been changing to a more humanistic attitude and the realisation that people do matter.

So the bosses, the managers, have had to learn the skills of managing, which include most importantly the art of working with people, the subject of this book.

First and foremost, and this applies in any walk of life, we have to learn how to communicate effectively. That means talking to people in an unthreatening way and at the appropriate level, so that they readily understand. It also means that we have to listen with empathy and ensure that we understand. So much of the confusion and conflict that arises in the workplace comes from poor communication. To communicate effectively is the most important thing the manager has to do. Without this all other aspects of the manager's job will be faulty – the job will get done, no doubt, but with unnecessary difficulty and rarely perfectly.

Leaders are indeed born, but even an ordinary person can be trained, moulded and guided into becoming an effective leader. We cannot all have charisma, flair and good looks, but we can all develop effective leadership. The leader (the manager) needs to build a team, a group of individuals with varying talents and abilities, who must blend together into a team to get the job done. Not an easy task because the leader will need to understand a good deal about people: be able to intuit character and recruit the best people to fit in the team to get the job done. The process of interviewing and selecting is a subtle one that the manager has to learn well and be most dispassionate about doing it. The wrong people in the team can, and probably will, be disruptive to the job and the stability of the team.

The manager cannot do all the work alone; there simply isn't enough time and time is a precious commodity that we all need to manage well. What the manager can do is to delegate part of the work (but not the ultimate responsibility). Delegation extends the manager's time and provides some opportunity for team members to develop their skills and develop their personal work horizon. Delegation, if done well, is highly motivational and is one of the areas in which the manager is in control. Some things that need to be done in any work situation will not be within the manager's control; this can be highly frustrating. Others, however, such as good and fair delegation can be used by the manager as a successful motivational tool. It is the manager's job to motivate their people and it is sensible to devote a good deal of effort to this because well-motivated people work well and produce the required results.

Problems are always on the manager's agenda; after all, that's your job, to solve problems – or is it? Problems, of whatever nature, are inevitable in management and some are intractable. But if you allow your people to let you solve problems for them you will be caught in the problem-solving trap. Encourage them, whenever possible, to bring you solutions, not problems. This system of 'outsourcing' problems is a good motivational factor as well as being developmental for your people; they feel they are contributing, this is great recognition.

Managers have to be planners, it is a given for the job. From taking part in the overall organisation, planning and strategy, to the detailed plan for their own section, the manager is deeply involved, and should involve the team too; they have valuable detailed knowledge of how to get the job done well. Planning involves scheduling of workflow; assignment of tasks to team members; calculating times and cash needs and so on. Plans need to be watched, if they are not producing the intended results they have to be changed. There is nothing more stupid in management than to continue with a plan that is no longer functioning. Part of the planning process is the scheduling of time for training and development of people. People's skills should be constantly refreshed and upgraded and, hopefully, innovative ideas will come out of training. An effective manager will encourage creative thinking from the team, which could result in better, more productive ways of doing the job.

Giving people opportunities for learning is an excellent way to motivate them. It really depends on what the individual wants; if they are ambitious they may want to learn new skills and aim for promotion; if they simply want to maintain their existing skills and performance, the manager should not press them, providing that their work is satisfactory. The manager's role is said to be 'to work myself out of a job'; so managers should encourage their people's efforts towards self-development. Again, this is good recognition of people and very motivational.

When working with people, there inevitably comes a time when something goes wrong: a team member steps out of line and seriously upsets or offends other people; or perhaps the company policy, or poor pay, or some other factor beyond your control gets the workforce into a rebellious frame of mind. However the situation arises, you may be faced with some unpleasant action; maybe you will have to discipline an individual or even deal with the legalistics of an arbitration tribunal. It is not the best part of a manager's life! But you are not alone; your company will have guidance, rules, handbooks and an HR department to support you. Likewise in any conflict situation, there will be ways of defusing the tension and with the full support of the HR people. Remember, it is not necessarily your fault that a conflict happens; what the manager should always try to do, is avoid conditions where a conflict can flare up. That means good management and best practice at all times. Easy to say but not always possible – we are, after all, only human.

One of the most time-consuming bugbears of management life is meetings. They are very necessary but can often be dispensed with. When we need to communicate widely, to consult, decide or inform, we need to gather people together at a specified time and place, with a programme (an agenda) to discuss, exchange views, and generally to decide some course of action. Unfortunately the arrangements are often poorly made, the discussion is pointless with perhaps a single person (the chairperson?) dominating the proceedings, and many of the participants contributing nothing at all. Meetings are so often a waste of time, but they need not be, if good preparation is made. This book will have given you some ideas of how to manage worthwhile meetings, and also how not to have them, and to communicate in other, more effective, ways. Management is working with people; to do this we need meetings. By following the precepts outlined you can ensure that your meetings are productive and not costly time-wasting ego exercises.

This book has given you an overview of what management is about. It is primarily about working with people to get things done. What those things are cover the whole spectrum of commercial and industrial life. Each business will have its specific objectives and expect to achieve its own specific outcomes. The inputs will vary infinitely in terms of resources required, but there is one common factor in everything that happens in business and that is the involvement of people. It doesn't really matter whether the business is a one-man band or a huge multinational, whether it operates in a sophisticated developed society or in a struggling developing economy, the common factor is that something has to get done and people do it. Working with people is the common thread. I hope that this book has shown some ways of making the whole cloth.

National Occupational Standards

Competency	Unit no.	Chapter	Chapter title
Develop productive working relationships with colleagues	D1	Chapter 2	How do we communicate?
		Chapter 5	How can you support your team?
		Chapter 6	How do you create learning opportunities?
		Chapter 7	How can you help people to develop?
		Chapter 8	How can you deal with conflict and problems and build a team?
		Chapter 11	How can you collaborate effectively?

Develop productive working relationships with colleagues and stakeholders	D2	Chapter 2	How do we communicate?
		Chapter 8	How can you deal with conflict and problems and build a team?
		Chapter 11	How can you collaborate effectively?
Recruit, select and keep colleagues	D3	Chapter 3	How do we recruit and select people?
		Chapter 5	How can you support your team?
		Chapter 6	How do you create learning opportunities?
		Chapter 7	How can you help people to develop?
		Chapter 8	How can you deal with conflict and problems and build a team?
Plan the workforce	D4	Chapter 1	Introduction
		Chapter 4	Why plan?
		Chapter 5	How can you support your team?
		Chapter 8	How can you deal with conflict and problems and build a team?
Allocate and check work in your team	D5	Chapter 2	How do we communicate?

(Continued)

		Chapter 5	How can you support your team?
		Chapter 7	How can you help people to develop?
		Chapter 8	How can you deal with conflict and problems and build a team?
		Chapter 11	How can you collaborate effectively?
Allocate and monitor the progress and quality of work in your area of responsibility	D6	Chapter 2	How do we communicate?
		Chapter 4	Why plan?
		Chapter 7	How can you help people to develop?
		Chapter 8	How can you deal with conflict and problems and build a team?
		Chapter 11	How can you collaborate effectively?
Provide learning opportunities for colleagues	D7	Chapter 3	How do we recruit and select people?
		Chapter 6	How do you create learning opportunities?
		Chapter 7	How can you help people to develop?

Help team members address problems affecting their performance	D8	Chapter 5	How can you support your team?
		Chapter 6	How do you create learning opportunities?
		Chapter 7	How can you help people to develop?
		Chapter 8	How can you deal with conflict and problems and build a team?
Build and manage teams	D9	Chapter 5	How can you support your team?
		Chapter 6	How do you create learning opportunities?
		Chapter 8	How can you deal with conflict and problems and build a team?
Reduce and manage conflict in your team	D10	Chapter 8	How can you deal with conflict and problems and build a team?
		Chapter 10	What are the best ways to solve disputes?
Lead meetings	D11	Chapter 9	What about meetings?
Participate in meetings	D12	Chapter 9	What about meetings?

(Continued)

Support individuals to develop and maintain their performance	D13	Chapter 2	How do we communicate?
		Chapter 5	How can you support your team?
		Chapter 6	How do you create learning opportunities?
		Chapter 7	How can you help people to develop?
		Chapter 8	How can you deal with conflict and problems and build a team?
Initiate and follow disciplinary procedure	D14	Chapter 10	What are the best ways to solve disputes?
Initiate and follow grievance procedure	D15	Chapter 10	What are the best ways to solve disputes?
Manage redundancies in your area of responsibility	D16	Chapter 8	How can you deal with conflict and problems and build a team?
		Chapter 10	What are the best ways to solve disputes?
Build and sustain collaborative relationships with other organisations	D17	Chapter 11	How can you collaborate effectively?

Further information and reading

Useful organisations and websites

Chartered Management Institute
Management House
Cottingham Road
Corby NN17 1TT
tel 01536 204222
www.managers.co.uk
For information about all aspects of management and management qualifications.

Management Standards Centre
3rd Floor, 2 Savoy Court
Strand
London WC2R 0EZ
tel: 0207 240 2826
www.management-standards.org/home

Department for Business Innovations and Skills
Ministerial Correspondence Unit
1 Victoria St
London SW1H 0EY
tel: 0207 215 5000
www.berr.gov.uk
For information about all aspects of business.

Official UK Government website
www.direct.gov.uk
For a wide variety of information including employment and education.

Office of Fair Trading
www.oft.gov.uk
For information on legislation affecting businesses.

Institute of Chartered Accountants in England and Wales
www.icaew.co.uk
For information on finance and accounting.

Chartered Institute of Marketing
www.marketinguk.co.uk
For information about market reports.

Chartered Institute of Personnel and Development
www.cipd.co.uk
For information on all aspects of Human Resource Management.

Business Link
tel: 0845 600 9006
www.businesslink.gov.uk
Business Link is a government-funded network of local advice centres for business.

Chambers of Commerce

www.chamberonline.co.uk
Local Chambers of Commerce are good sources of information on
a variety of local and national business matters.

Investors in People

helpline 0207 467 1946
www.investorsinpeople.co.uk

British Retail Consortium

www.brc.org.uk
For information about retail selling.

Institute of Business Consulting

Helpline 01536 207480

Learndirect

www.leamdirect-business.com
For advice about all sorts of business training and courses.

Small Firms Enterprise and Development Initiative

www.sfedi.co.uk
Tel: 0114 241 2155

Further reading

If you wish to further explore the ideas of management development and working with people, you will have a difficult time. There is so much material, and more is being added daily (this book included). There is truth in all the books in the following list; I have my own favourites which have influenced my thinking and development. I have found them useful, idea rich, occasionally inspiring and above all, readable. Much that has been recently published is worth reading; this list deals with fundamentals of management theory. One needs to have a good foundation before going into deeper waters. This list will help build that good foundation.

R. M. Belbin, *Management Teams,* Elsevier, 2010

Sidney Callis, *Business Writing, A guide to doing it well*, Management Books 2000 Ltd, 2008

Peter Drucker, *The Effective Executive*, HarperCollins 1993

Adrian Furnham, *People Management In Turbulent Times*, Palgrave Macmillan, 2009

Charles Handy, *Gods of Management*, Pan Books, 1995

Frederick Herzberg, *Work and the Nature of Man*, World Publishing, 1973

W. B. Johnson and C. R. Ridley, *The Elements of Mentoring*, Palgrave Macmilllan, 2004

Mike Leibling, *Working With The Enemy*, Kogan Page, 2009

Henry Mintzberg, *The Nature of Managerial Work*, Harper & Row, 1997

Bob Selden, *What To Do When You Become The Boss*, Outskirts Press, 2007

Index